COACH'S CORNER

WINNING AT WORK

Professional and career development advice scored from coaching youth sports

TROY STEVENSON

ISBN: 979-8-9885327-0-5 (paperback)
ISBN: 979-8-9885327-1-2 (hardcover)

TABLE OF CONTENTS

INTRODUCTION

Growing up, I was a mediocre athlete at best. I played lots of sports—baseball, soccer, tennis, basketball, you name it. I worked hard. I practiced a lot. I poured my heart into it. But over time, it became evident that my dream of launching a walk-off homer over the wall in Wrigley Field to win the World Series just wasn't going to pan out. In hindsight, the root causes of my limitations were fairly simple: I was too small and not particularly coordinated. The mantel in our house displayed a lot more participation ribbons than "Most Valuable Player" trophies. As my childhood wound down, I packed up my assorted cleats, balls and pungent jerseys and turned my attention to other pursuits and ways to compete.

Luckily, I was better at *business* than I was at sports. Over time, I climbed the proverbial corporate ladder. For the past two decades, I've been an executive at three prominent Bay Area tech companies. My lack of speed, coordination and size didn't hold me back in the corporate arena. Success was more a function of being good at math, meetings and processes—things that were more in my wheelhouse. But I never stopped wishing I could be out on the field hearing the roar of the crowd rather than in a conference room answering tough questions from other executives and business partners.

Although I loved watching pro athletes compete on the field and on TV, I seldom thought much about youth sports or little leagues until one fateful day when my then seven-year-old daughter signed up to play soccer for our local recreational league. Her decision to join a team triggered a series of increasingly desperate and pleading emails from the league office about the need for parents to help out on the field. I learned that when a bunch of parents drop off their precocious offspring at the park on a Saturday afternoon, the kids don't naturally line up in formation and commence drills. Rather, the scene quickly degrades into chaos as dozens of excitedly unsupervised children commence to rolling around in the grass, wandering off, singing jingles or crying for Mommy to come back. And that's where the coaches (a.k.a. babysitters) come in. Coaches bring order to the chaos and try to generate at least a few minutes of kids actually kicking a soccer ball before snack time.

I was hooked. Being a helper and a coach was actually super fun. And it was a nice break from my day job of responding to customer complaints, writing slides for presentations, sending emails and attending meetings. The kids actually listened to what I said. At least sometimes. It was rewarding to feel that I was teaching new skills, developing young minds and wiping away tears from every new *owie*.

Who knows, maybe I was even playing a small role in developing a future superstar. But most of all, I enjoyed this high-quality time with my daughter, her friends and some other equally clueless parent-coaches. Not a bad way to spend a weekend and get out of doing household chores.

What started as a reluctant response to a pleading email became kind of an obsession. Over the next decade, I served as a volunteer coach, assistant, manager, referee, team parent and general manager for a wide variety of sports teams that my two kids were involved in. The sports ranged from those I knew a decent bit about, such as soccer and baseball, to those that I had to learn before I could teach. During one period when I was unexpectedly unemployed, I coached my kids' middle school track-and-field team to a lackluster but rewarding season.

I discovered that the gene for athletic prowess sometimes skips a generation, as both of my kids were much more successful athletes than I ever was, particularly at sports that required speed and agility. Coaching became a way for me to attain, via proxy, the childhood glory I had dreamed of but never achieved. Coaching rekindled my competitive streak, sometimes for better and sometimes for worse.

On the sidelines, I tried to stay calm and positive, but sometimes my emotions ran high and I gave a poor teenaged referee a piece of my mind. I'm thankful that cell phone cameras and social media sites weren't ubiquitous during much of my coaching career. As my kids got older and started to join "real teams" led by "real coaches," I reflected back on my involvement with youth sports as a great way to spend time with my kids, make a small difference in the community and have some fun. But I also thought that was probably the extent of it.

And then came Uber. I joined the company as it was entering global hyper-growth across multiple businesses in virtually every corner of the world. My job was to build, scale and run our global customer support, driver onboarding, safety response, account management and back-office organization, collectively known as Community Operations or CommOps. My role quickly grew to overseeing tens of thousands of people spread across hundreds of locations and speaking dozens of languages. It challenged every aspect of my management playbook. The only way for me to lead an organization of such a massive scale was to try to be more of a coach than a manager. And the only way to build relationships, communicate ideas and develop teams across such a far-flung enterprise 24 hours a day, seven days a week and 365 days a year was to do so virtually. And so I started to write.

I wrote about the many ways in which what I'd learned from coaching and managing youth sports teams helped to inform how I approached my "real job" of leading adults and teams in the business world. The parallels were numerous, sometimes surprising, and fun to explore. Before I knew it, what started as a simple set of emails I'd sent to my management team grew virally into a companywide leadership coaching blog that's been distributed to tens of thousands of Uber employees across every part of the company. It also became a way for me to build my own professional brand at Uber and scale my ability to develop people and drive a coaching-based culture. I called these blog posts "Coach's Corner."

One of the goals I had on my bucket list for a long time was to write a book. I couldn't be more excited to bring this labor of love to fruition, and I hope you'll enjoy reading about my 30-plus years of accumulated business and athletic coaching foibles, lessons and anecdotes. I hope you'll appreciate these stories, pick up a few handy tips and find some inspiration for how you can be a more effective coach in any of your life's endeavors.

PLAYING WITHOUT A PLAYBOOK

Coaching a Little League baseball team can be surprisingly stressful. You might think the primary focus would be teaching kids how to catch, throw and swing, but the job actually requires a diverse mix of skills, including project management, psychology, linear programming, security (i.e., dealing with unruly parents in the bleachers), childcare and supply chain analysis. Managing Uber's Community Operations' global workforce of tens of thousands can be stressful, but it's a cakewalk compared to managing a dozen menacing ten-year-olds. And the planning and logistics involved in baseball can be just as complex.

I learned this the hard way several years ago as a rookie coach for my son's baseball team. I was super nervous about our first game, so I spent a ton of time planning for it. In youth baseball, *planning* means setting a batting order and figuring out which kid will play which fielding position in each inning.

What makes the planning so complex is:

- Constructing a lineup that is not only competitive, i.e., playing to win, but also ensures all the kids will develop skills and have a positive experience.
- Balancing each kid's preferences with safety considerations. For example, many kids want to play first base, but an *attention-span-challenged first baseman* is likely to lose some teeth.
- League rules require that each kid, regardless of skill level, must play a prescribed number of innings in the infield and get the same number of at-bats.
- The fact that every parent has an inflated view of his or her offspring's talents and a strong opinion about how the coach should manage the team. Many of these parents are also your neighbors and friends, at least on non-game-days.

Going into the first game of the season I thought I had the perfect plan laid out in detail on my clipboard. I was confident that my hours of meticulous analysis, orchestration and logistical innovation would be rewarded. Not to brag, but I had a master's degree in Operations Management. How hard could developing a winning Little League game plan be, for heck's sake? I knew where each of my twelve kids would play in each of our six innings. My plan would ensure that each kid would get a chance to play his favorite position at least once, each inning's defensive scheme would have my stars strategically sprinkled across the diamond, everyone would have fun, the parents wouldn't whine too much about their precious progeny being treated unfairly, and perhaps we'd even win the game. Easy!

Game time arrived, and my meticulous plan unwound before the first pitch was thrown. I never got to implement step one. Instead I had to manage through confusion, chaos, crisis and even a bit of crying.

- Two kids, including my best player, were surprise no-shows because they had schedule conflicts their parents had forgot to inform me about. So my lineup card was obsolete.
- I lost another player in the first inning when he got stung by a bee in the outfield and wanted to sit with his mommy in the bleachers for the rest of the game.
- In the second inning, we were clearly outmatched and losing 0-8. Perhaps the other coach was sneaking twelve-year-old-ringers into his line-up! But I resisted the urge to ask to see their birth certificates.
- About an hour into the game, a thunderstorm rolled in. After the fourth inning, the umpire called everything off.

My plan was never implemented. But I did learn an important lesson. The hours I'd put into **the planning process** turned out to be super useful in helping me manage the actual game. By *doing the planning,* I'd forced myself to better understand things like game strategy, player strengths and weaknesses, competitive positioning and resource optimization. And these skills served me well to dynamically manage the team through the rest of the season, regardless of what bizarre new calamity befell us each week. Little did I know then that I would learn this lesson again years later at Uber.

Here's how things played out in Community Operations over one month in 2020:

- Each of our major Community Operations facilities historically had a robust business continuity plan (BCP) filed away. BCPs contemplated what we'd do to keep serving customers if we had to close a site for a few days due to an earthquake in San Francisco or a typhoon in Manila, for example. They didn't contemplate what we'd do if everything closed down all at once.
- Then we started hearing about this strange new sickness, a novel coronavirus, later known as Covid-19, that was springing up in a handful of cities. Things started accelerating from there.
- It became clear we needed a plan. So in early March, several Community Operations leaders spent a few days together at what turned out to be our last in-person meeting, thinking through various scenarios and what we should be doing to plan for them.
- From there, we launched a bunch of sub-teams to flesh out a variety of plans for how we'd manage things like employee exposures, site outages, containment solutions, customer response scenarios, technology needs and so on. All of these plans contemplated gradual and sporadic impacts in a few of our more than 700 centers around the world. Most relied on shifting work across the global network.

- Collectively, our teams spent hundreds of hours in planning. We felt pretty good about the thoroughness, actionability and robustness of our plans. Although the plans had come together quickly, they seemed solid.
- Then, over the course of just a few days, pretty much the entire world shut down. Almost 100% of our offices and BPO facilities were hastily closed.
- We hadn't planned for that—or anything even remotely close to that. Such a scenario wasn't even deemed within the realm of possibility since it had never happened before in the history of the world.

Yet even though we didn't have an *actual plan* that was appropriate for what happened, we somehow managed to:

- Transition about 30,000 customer support agents to a work-from-home ("WFH") model, most of whom had never done so before and didn't even have the technology needed for WFH.
- Launched myriad tech enhancements to automate, redirect and prioritize the flood of customer inbound requests that were swamping our severely diminished capacity.
- Continuously and dynamically reprioritized customer support queues to ensure we were deploying our available staff to handle the most urgent customer needs, massively ramp up capacity across the UberEats onboarding funnel, etc.
- Adapted our myriad people policies, training, QA and team management approaches to enable customer support

personnel to work from tens of thousands of unique locations (often at home, with limited internet bandwidth or connectivity).

- And that was only a small part of the overall list. And that was just in week one.

Much like with my Little League baseball coaching experience, *our plans* were quickly abandoned when real-life intervened. But the *process of planning* was invaluable, and worth every minute of the hours the teams had spent developing the actual plans that we didn't use.

Here's why the planning process was so important. It:

- Helped us build muscle in some of the key areas we'd need to flex throughout the crisis.
- Forced us to think through myriad scenarios and the implications of each one.
- Served as the impetus to build cross-functional teams and figure out new ways of working together effectively.
- Prepared us for the discussions we'd need to have with our internal and external business partners to arrive at workable solutions in real time as the world changed.
- Provided us with a head start on some of the technology and people-enablement processes that proved critical as we closed sites.
- Gave us the confidence to take bold actions to try to get ahead of the count each time life threw us a curveball.

So my advice is to have a plan for anything that is important in your professional and personal life. Invest the time to make sure the plan is robust, complete and actionable. Refine your plans often. Share them with your colleagues. You might never need the plans. And if you do, they might not work. But by forcing yourself to *do the planning*, you'll be more likely to achieve your dreams, or at least help a Little League baseball team avoid embarrassment.

POSITIONING YOUR TEAM TO WIN

Randomness influences the outcome of most sporting events. Balls take funny bounces, referees make mistakes, weather changes, star players get grounded for teasing their siblings, and luck intervenes in a variety of ways. As a result, the best player or team doesn't always win. And that's a good thing because sports would be boring if the outcomes were preordained based entirely on which team is better *on paper*.

However for a coach, this randomness can be frustrating. You can't swing the bat yourself. You can't control every element of the game. You can't plan for every contingency. All that you can do is put your team in the best possible position to win and then hope for the best.

Here are some tips I've learned from coaching. No single factor can guarantee a championship, but taken together, they can certainly boost the odds. It mostly boils down to *control what you can control*:

- **Assemble the right team:** Build a team with a diverse mix of talents and experiences. Don't over-index on just the most visible or obvious attributes. Tom Brady is the greatest player in the history of football, but a team of eleven Tom Brady's would get slaughtered. You need the right player for each position and reasonable depth to cover for injuries. It's also important to build a team with good chemistry and players who play together well, even if that means letting go of superstar primadonnas.

- **Optimize your lineup:** Having the right team isn't enough. You then need to get the right players in the right positions. The biggest pain point as a Little League coach is that every kid wants to play pitcher. But most can't. You've got to put players in positions where they can succeed and help the team win. It's also important to balance things so you don't leave gaps or burn out stars.
- **Get in shape:** You aren't always going to have the best team and talent is not equally distributed, but you can have the team with the best work ethic and conditioning. In the words of Herb Brooks, legendary coach from *Miracle on Ice*, "I can't promise you we'll be the best team at Lake Placid next February, but we will be the best conditioned. That I can promise you. Again!" Make sure you teach your players the fundamentals and instill values like hard work, hustle and a will to win.
- **Have a plan:** In my son's first year playing flag football, he and his friends were too young to read playbooks, so they only had one play, which was *everyone go out for a pass and try to get open.* Over time, they developed playbooks,

complex routes and even some trick plays. By the time the kids were big enough to beat the parents, the only way to win was to have a sophisticated and nuanced plan of attack. (Note: it is unclear whether the teenagers beat their dads due to the brilliant playbooks or the fact that they were scrimmaging against a bunch of guys well past their primes.)

- **...but be flexible:** A good coach also needs to know when to scrap the playbook. Be introspective enough to realize when it's just not working. Sometimes your team might fall so far behind that they need to start flinging it deep or get so far ahead that the smart move is to run out the clock. Or you lose a key player and have to quickly revise the plan to something the backup can execute.
- **Work the angles:** Don't cheat, of course, but that doesn't mean you can't adapt your game to reality. When a ref is lazy about offside calls, I send my girls on earlier runs. Except when we're defending, in which case, our sideline is vocally "helping" that same ref realize when our opponents are offside.
- **Know your competition:** Your team accounts for only half the players on the field at any time. So if you want to win, you better know a lot about the folks out there standing in your way. What are their strengths, vulnerabilities and blind spots? What is their strategy likely to be and how can you counter it? What can you do to neutralize their relative strengths and competitive advantages?

- **When you're the weaker team:** You need to keep the score close enough so that you have a chance to get lucky or seize on a mistake. You also want to add an element of unpredictability, so that you introduce more randomness and the outcome becomes less reliant on pure size or skill. If I'm coaching the weaker team, I'm hoping for gusty winds and a slippery field. Also, when you're up against a fierce team that has been consistently beating you, you need to avoid the temptation to just emulate their strategy and tactics to close the gap. It probably won't work since you have a different (possibly worse) team. Rather, trap them into playing your game, a strategy pioneered by Ali in the Rumble In The Jungle.
- **When you're the stronger team:** Keep using your superior size, strength or speed to your advantage. Leverage your scale and depth. Stick to the fundamentals, but try to strike hard early to demoralize your opponent and not leave things to chance. And don't get lazy. In the words of basketball star Kevin Durant "Hard work beats talent when talent fails to work hard."

Doing everything on this list won't win you every game. But by putting your team in the best possible position to succeed, you'll win more than your fair share. And that's how great coaches build legacies. I'm not sure any of this has much to do with how to win the global rideshare or food delivery business, but it's all I got. Go team!

KEEPING SCORE

Confession: I have an unhealthy (and probably unnatural) love of metrics, goals and, especially, a type of strategic management method known as "Balanced Scorecards." If my wife hadn't vetoed the idea repeatedly, I'd raise our kids using a Balanced Scorecard. We'd have key performance indicators ("KPIs") for academics, chores, behavior and attitude–with weekly drill-downs.

One of the first things I did upon taking the helm of Community Operations was to put in place a Balanced Scorecard. We start every operating review by diagnosing it.

Why do I love our Community Operations Balanced Scorecard?

- It clearly illustrates the things we believe are most critical to our success (e.g., quality, efficiency, safety and employee engagement). And it does so in a way that we can share with thousands of teammates and business partners around the world.
- It enables us to set goals and hold ourselves accountable.

- It gives us smart ways to probe on key performance drivers. Honestly, I don't care that much about lines moving up or down. What I focus on is **why** things happened, what we learned and if or if so how we need to course-correct.
- It creates healthy friction because we need to exercise judgment and make tradeoffs. It prevents us from over-indexing on one priority at the expense of others. For example, simultaneously optimizing our customer support to deliver both high quality and efficient cost.
- It makes it clear to every employee how they impacted the success of our function. Every person, project and action should contribute in some way to achieving our goals.
- And to quote management guru Peter Drucker, "What gets measured gets managed, and what gets managed gets done."

But I worry we sometimes have a problem with how we tend to use Balanced Scorecards. Let me explain, and I'll do so via the lens of a basketball team.

In basketball, there is a scoreboard. And it provides critical KPIs for the coach and team. Without it, they don't know how they're doing. (e.g., are they winning or losing? How much time do they have left to shoot?)

But you don't win a game by obsessing about the scoreboard. You win by having a great strategy, training hard, getting the best talent on the court, executing the right plays, exploiting your competitor's weaknesses and correcting quickly when things don't work. It also helps to have LeBron James on your roster.

The scorecard is an important guide. For example, is our game plan working? Is everyone on the team contributing? Do we need to hurry up or slow down? The scorecard is a snapshot of a moment in time. It tells you more about the "what" than it tells you about the "why." And it never tells you what to do next. It's an end, not a means.

Over-focusing on short-term scorecard movements can be frustrating, misleading and counterproductive. Good KPIs are highly indicative of success over time. However, trying to explain small movements over short time periods is not. If you're not careful, you'll waste a lot of time trying to do so and that will come at the expense of things you could be doing to actually win the game.

So glance at the scorecard frequently throughout the game. But don't stare at it too long. Focus on the fundamentals of your team and the game.

My advice:

- Figure out the KPIs that matter most to your team or function. Define them clearly. Set goals. Make them visible.
- Ensure that your Balanced Scorecard has an element of healthy friction across the KPIs and that it forces nuanced thinking. Success is about making good trade offs with finite resources.

- Make sure you understand how your KPIs tie to your manager's and your function's. Know how your KPIs ladder up to your organization's. If they don't tie and ladder well, rethink them.
- Obsess about the numbers, but only from the perspective of what you're learning from them and how you can take action as a result, not just whether they're green or red.
- Remember that metrics are merely a means to an end. Manage them, but don't let them manage you. If you're not applying judgment, wisdom and insight to actioning "the data," it is only a matter of time before your job will be done by future robot overlords (i.e., ChatGPT).

KNOWING YOURSELF

The most common and cliche leadership platitudes I often hear is "just be yourself." That's a nice sentiment, but it isn't very helpful. And it's certainly incomplete.

Rather, I think a key to effective leadership isn't just being yourself, but rather, *knowing yourself*. And even more importantly, helping others *know you*.

Knowing yourself sounds easy, right? After all, if you're not an expert on yourself, then who is? But how often do you really put yourself under a microscope and dissect what makes you tick? You should do that more often. Here's why.

First, this self-examination will make you more aware of your inner preferences, motivations, styles and patterns. With that knowledge, you can leverage your strengths and work on your gaps. That's the obvious part, though.

More important, your employees and teammates are eager to know the real you. Your values. Your preferences. Your aspirations. And every possible tip and trick about how to succeed with you. You are their manager and as such, you play a big role not only in their jobs, but also their lives.

Believe it or not, you are a super interesting person to them!

So why keep your teams guessing? It's much better to open up and let your teams get to know you. There is nothing like disclosure to build trust. Plus, you'll probably find that by opening up to your employees, they'll open up more to you. And this will enable you to be an even better manager for them. Everybody wins!

So how do you help people know you better? Lots of ways. You should seek your own genuine path. Personally, I find it kind of awkward to talk a lot about myself, and I much prefer to write about myself. Writing lets me be structured and clear, and not forget important stuff. Writing about myself isn't a substitute for interpersonal interactions, but it is rather additive.

A few years ago I took some time to study myself and then I wrote a handy guide, "Working with Troy - A User's Manual," (an idea I proudly plagiarized from a former manager and mentor) that I share with every new direct report I hire and sometimes with my colleagues. And then I ask, but don't require, that they do the same for me.

Here's the current version of my guide. You can use it as a template to write your own personal user's manual. Carve out some time this week to think about yourself and how you can share more of yourself with your teams.

Working with Troy - A User's Manual (v93.6)

Some stuff about me that's not on my resume:

- I grew up in Missouri in a large blended family with five kids and two dogs. This was long before smartphones, so much of my childhood was spent outside and unsupervised.
- My dad was a small business owner. Like all entrepreneurs, he experienced highs and lows. I've always been proud of the way he provided for his family and the lessons he imparted to us about the value of personal reputation, risk-taking and hustling. I spent summers working on a factory floor.
- I've been married to my college sweetheart, Barb, for over twenty-five years. We have two kids, Steph and Zach, and an lovable, but mischievous dog, Myko. Prior to the kids recently heading off to college, most of my free time and weekends typically involved sports and kids' activities. I'm also an avid road biker.
- Of all the titles I've had, "Coach" is among the most meaningful to me. I've coached youth soccer, baseball and track. I love watching kids develop their skills and understanding of the game. I love competition, although I sometimes need to tone this down. I like to think some of the coaching skills I learned through sports translate into how I coach at work.

How I'm wired:

- I believe great companies are obsessed with the actual customer experiences that they provide. They infuse customer-centricity into their culture. I've been a super-user of every company I've worked for and expect the same of my teams. You need to eat your own cooking.
- I like things to be well-structured. I feel more comfortable when I know there's a plan. When faced with ambiguity, my first impulse is to clarify and structure, and I'm uneasy until this is accomplished. I believe in prioritization and focus, and I make concerted efforts to identify top priorities. I think we can all have the biggest impact by doing a few things exceptionally well.
- I like to start most tasks with the end in mind and work backwards. That doesn't mean that the final answer won't change, but rather that we begin with clear hypotheses supported by logical work-streams.
- I'm pretty hands-on when it comes to analytics, problem-solving and communications. This sometimes strikes others as a lack of trust. Please give me the benefit of the doubt that if I'm digging into something, it is because I'm interested and want to help.
- I'm a fairly easy-going person and have a dry and self-deprecating sense of humor. Sometimes this comes across as being disengaged. That is seldom actually the case.
- I'm a bit introverted. I form strong relationships over time and they are critical to my job satisfaction. I have

maintained longterm friendships with most of my former managers, peers and direct reports.

How I try to work:

- I enjoy working collaboratively. I have a preference for consensus and buy-in and I'm willing to take the time to get there, when that's possible. I like hearing different points of view, but once a decision is made, I expect us all to own it.
- I think people are generally well-intentioned and want to do the right thing. When an interaction or comment rubs me the wrong way, my first impulse is to assume I am misinterpreting the comment and seek to clarify it. I appreciate being given the same courtesy.
- Similarly, I tend to trust people until proven otherwise. The best way to build trust with me is to be clear about your commitments and then deliver on them. I realize that timelines and priorities sometimes change, but I hate late surprises.
- I don't like to leave things hanging or feel that there is festering resentment in a relationship. My preference is for candid feedback and open dialogue about how to resolve conflict quickly. I don't hold grudges, nor do I expect others to.
- I am very open to feedback and work hard to act on it. Please don't be bashful about sharing feedback with me, whether it's positive or not. It's how I learn. Similarly, I am candid about giving feedback.

Some pet peeves:

- I value logical and well-thought-out problem-solving. It's the best way to convince me of your point of view. When I don't understand the reasoning behind someone's conclusion, I tend to resist it. I find data and facts to be powerful persuaders. I want to see the numbers.
- I quickly lose confidence in people when I believe they are undermining the group, not supporting one another or becoming overly focused on their personal agendas.
- Slide decks are often how we communicate and drive action. Thus, it is critical that your decks are clear, well-structured and persuasive. I promise I will annoy you on this topic.
- Punctuality matters. It demonstrates basic courtesy and respect. Ditto for not multitasking when you're interacting with others.

How I like to communicate:

- I like to use email for tactical communications and updates. I consider email to be akin to a conversation, in that I will be highly responsive and timely and I expect the same from others.
- I provide better guidance when I've had time to think things through in advance rather than try to process them in real-time. I appreciate getting materials in advance and will make an effort to pre-read and have my thoughts ready.

LEARNING FROM LOSING

When my youngest kid headed off to high school, my coaching career sadly came to an end. From that point on, my kids had real coaches instead of an aging hyper-competitive dad trying to live vicariously through his progeny....So I was in a reflective mood.

Over the years, the teams I've coached have accumulated some great wins and many painful losses. And although the wins were more fun, we learned more from the losses. The losses taught us about our team, areas in which we needed to improve, flaws in our game plans, and most importantly, our characters. Losses teach resilience. Losses plant seeds.

When your team wins, you celebrate. And you immediately start thinking about the next game. Those aren't exactly ideal conditions for earnest introspection and learning.

But when teams lose, they don't celebrate. Rather, the losing coaches reflect and immediately start thinking about what they could have done differently. That creates ideal conditions for true insight.

The first thing a coach has to learn is how to be a good

loser. It may be tempting to take out your emotions on the players. To yell at those who performed poorly or made mistakes. This might help you feel better in the moment, but you'll be berating your players when they're most vulnerable. They'll start pointing fingers at one another, further eroding the team's chemistry. Some might even quit the team. You'll lose the opportunity to learn from the loss and you'll create conditions in which the loss will beget more losses.

After a painful loss, I try to skip the immediate post-mortem and instead congratulate the other coach, console the kids and thank the parents. I give myself some time to emotionally recharge.

Then I ask myself some questions:

- Was the problem one of strategy or tactics and how might we have approached things differently?
- Did we understand our competitor well enough and did we anticipate and prepare for the situations we encountered?
- Did we have the right team on the field, the right players in the right positions, adapt our tactics as the situations evolved?
- What should we have done differently and what kept us from realizing it at the time?
- What do we need to improve to increase our likelihood of success going forward?

Uber has done a crazy lot of winning in our short history. Perhaps we got so used to winning that we weren't prepared for some of the painful losses of 2017. We didn't learn from them as much as we might have. And we didn't handle them as well as we could have. That needed to change if we were going to build a true dynasty with championship banners hanging from the rafters.

Although I'm pleased overall with our win-loss record in Community Operations, there have been some tough losses over the past few years. We've learned from them and we're stronger as a result.

For example:

- Our results in our annual employee satisfaction survey, known internally as "Pulse," a few years ago were terrible, but we didn't hang our heads in defeat. Instead, we diagnosed the problems, developed plans and tweaked our line-up. And we put up one heck of a score in the last round.
- Several years ago, we made some mistakes in our safety support function. The press stories were brutal. But we didn't point fingers. Instead, we hustled and reinvented virtually everything. Today, we have the most robust capabilities in the industry.
- In the U.S. a few years ago Lyft beat us by five points on a driver cSAT survey. So we analyzed, course-corrected and executed. Most recently, we notched a big win on that same survey. That said, we still have many opportunities for improvement, so nobody better be spiking the ball anytime soon!

Uber competes against some of the most fearsome and talented companies in history. And we live in an increasingly competitive world. Everyone loses sometimes in sports, in life and in business. If you never lose, you're probably not challenging yourself enough. You're playing it too safe. You won't learn or grow.

I'm not trying to glorify losing. Losing sucks. Lose too many games, and even the best coaches get fired. Luckily for me, that's less of a risk when you're coaching 12-year-olds. Winning is much better. But the best way to win more often is to learn from every loss and to celebrate the times you played hard, but came up short.

ON WINNING

I love to win. It's an obsession I try to keep contained since I'm usually coaching kids.

Uber has done a ton of winning. We've built one of the world's most iconic companies *overnight*. We've overcome fierce competition and seemingly insurmountable barriers. We've put huge numbers on the board. We've won. A lot.

I joined Uber in 2016, eager to be part of such a winning juggernaut. There have been some sweet victories, most notably how we got through what felt like an existential crisis (a bunch of them actually) in late 2017, and set up our company on a much more sound and sustainable foundation. And I'm super proud of our Community Operations' wins in such areas as defect reduction, safety, and employee engagement.

You can tell who is winning a game by looking at the scoreboard. But in business, you can't simply count up the goals or runs scored. It's not always clear what the scoreboard even actually is. Stock price? Category positions? Profits? On each of those measures, I'm sure we'd all like to see ourselves winning more consistently than we have. It's hard to ignore that our competitors are also playing to win and sometimes they win at our expense.

In sports, when a team wants to win more, they start asking themselves some tough questions. For example:

- Winning requires **confronting hard truths**. and being willing to change the game plan if it's not working. Winning teams look forward, not backward. No team, no matter how strong its track record is, is *entitled* to win. The team has to earn that win every time. The goals the team scored in the last game get reset to zero when the next game starts.
- A manager has to assess if she has **the right team** on the field and the right players in the optimal positions. If not, she has to change things up, tweak the lineups, add new talent to fill gaps and make other improvements. These are some of the hardest decisions a manager has to make, but they're also some of the most impactful.
- Teams that win championships have consistent attitudes, particularly as they relate to **shared purposes and teamwork**. They drink the kool-aid. They share a common goal: winning. Every player is striving to win a championship banner, not a most-valuable-player trophy.
- Winning teams know the competition inside and out. They watch the game films. They anticipate the moves competitors are going to make and they stay one step ahead of them. They **play fair, but they dish out a lot of hard tackles.**

- Winners **put in the hours**. Winning teams outwork their competition. NFL great Jerry Rice famously said, "I do things in practice that other players won't do so that I can do things in games that other players can't do." My biggest lesson from coaching is that the most talented team often wins the game, but the team that hustles, works hardest and *wants it the most* usually wins the championship.

There is only a one letter difference between "winning" and "whining." I've never been part of a team, regardless of their talent level, that consistently did the former while doing much of the latter. And candidly, I sometimes get the sense that we're all becoming a bit too whiny. Things aren't perfect anywhere. I'm not saying you shouldn't speak up when you feel aggrieved. But first, ask yourself if your energy wouldn't be better focused on building and self-improvement, rather than dwelling on the negatives or complaining about the refs. Winning company cultures overcome the same challenges that losing company cultures whine about.

Winning isn't everything. All teams go through cycles. We're not going to win every game, but we need to start winning more often and more consistently. I want to win and I want *the scoreboard* to reflect that. In our stock price. In our category position. In our profitability. But most important, in our culture. I'm confident that we have the team, capabilities and fundamentals that we need to win a lot. It is in our hands. Let's win. Now play ball!

MANAGING YOUR CAREER

There's (probably) no such thing as the Career Fairy. But luckily, career management is easy. Every 2.36 years, you'll get promoted, typically to your boss's role when she gets promoted to the next level. And then you retire. The perfect plan! **Except that's not how it usually works.**

Take me, for example. I have a job that I love leading a critical function at one of the world's coolest companies. I did a quick self-study to figure out how this happened. The answer might surprise you:

- In 25 years, I've been promoted five times. That's once every five years. Hardly the rocket ship of expectations that seems prevalent at Uber.
- But some interesting things happened in the gaps between my celebratory promotion dinners:
    - Seven times I took on substantial additional responsibilities without getting promoted. More work, same title. Bad deal? Perhaps. But it was a great way to develop new skills and relationships.

  - Five times I made a lateral move to a completely different role. Starting over? Maybe. But it helped me learn what I was good at and what I enjoyed.
  - Three times I was "layered" into what seemed like a lower position. Upsetting? Maybe for a few days. But I kept an open mind and ended up learning a lot from my new manager and forging important new relationships.
  - Twice my role was eliminated. Scary? You bet! But in both cases it ended up being for the best for me personally and professionally.
  - Of my five promotions, only one was directly into my manager's job.

Throughout this journey, I've learned some things you may find helpful:

- Don't chase levels or titles. Not because they aren't important. I won't pretend that money and prestige don't matter. However, chasing titles is the worst way to actually get them. That will artificially narrow your focus and limit your opportunities. And if you're not careful, it will irritate your managers, who may come to see you as self-serving.
- Be open to lateral moves that build your skills and expand your network. You should be doing this whenever you feel you're starting to stagnate. Collect skills and experiences, not titles. Think of titles as the outcomes of lateral moves.

- Be a peer leader. Be the person who actively shares and cross-pollinates. Be the coach. Be *a* leader, even when you're not *the* leader. Leaders above you will start to perceive you as more senior than you are. At some point, promoting you will just seem logical and intuitive. #sneaky
- Take on more. Even when more work doesn't come with a bigger title or paycheck, find important things that aren't getting done and volunteer to do them. Figure out what your boss doesn't have time or expertise to focus on and ask her if you can help.
- Look around, not just straight up. Expect to take a few sidesteps for every step up. Those sidesteps are important because they build your skills and network. And you're working the odds. By demonstrating proficiency in multiple areas, you have better odds that a more senior role for which you're qualified will open up over time. #math
- Don't apply for every job that pops up just because it's a level above yours. I've made this mistake a couple of times and it damaged my relationships and credibility. Your motivations quickly become apparent and people will begin to distrust your judgment and intentions.
- Play the long game. Your career is likely to span forty-plus years. You're going to have lulls and even some setbacks. #relax
- Yes, titles and promotions are great, but do stuff that makes you happy and inspires you. You'll enjoy your job,

and more important, your life, more. And you're more likely to shine at it and end up getting promoted as a result. #irony

Manage your career well and you might end up becoming CEO someday. And when that happens, please remember the folks who gave you the advice that helped you get there!

BEING A GOOD OPERATOR

You know who's one heck of a good operator? An inspirational leader adored by all? Someone I've always considered a role model? **Santa.** The guy operates at a vast scale, orchestrating billions of deliveries across virtually every corner of the globe and navigating byzantine customs' rules, thorny labor relations and animal welfare laws. He runs a highly seasonal business with the vast majority of deliveries occurring on a single night. And he's developed complex algorithms to differentiate his offerings based on who's been naughty and who's been nice. We can all learn a lot from Santa about what it means to be an operational leader.

Community Operations is one of the most operational parts of Uber. Every week, we serve millions of customers with hundreds of different types of issues in dozens of languages. We process tens of millions of documents, menus and forms that keep the business safe and compliant. We coordinate the work of tens of thousands of front-line team members. It's not quite Santa-level volumes, but we do it without the benefit of magical flying reindeer.

Being an operational leader isn't about directly managing (or even just being aware of) every detail of a vast operation. It's about ensuring that the right *conditions* are in place to drive results. In the words of legendary football coach John Popovich, "As their coach, your job is to set the bar high, inspire them to reach this bar, encourage them, and most of all, guide them in the best possible manner and in the most supportive environment."

Whether you are leading large teams in an Operations Center, managing a small group of high-powered analysts or doing critical work as an individual contributor to enable your company's operations to be successful, there are some tactics you can deploy to be an effective *operator*.

- **Define clear success objectives:** Santa doesn't just hop on his sleigh and start randomly dumping Legos and dolls down chimneys. The first rule of being a good operator is having well-thought-out and clearly articulated objectives, and then fleshing out each objective into a tangible plan.
- **Create a Balanced Scorecard:** You need continuous insights into how things are going, so it's essential to have an actionable dashboard. I'm a fan of the Balanced Scorecard approach because it creates "intentional friction" between KPIs, which helps drive optimization and discipline. For example, our Community Operations Balanced Scorecard includes KPIs that measure both cSAT and Cost - factors that are often in conflict with each other. By managing to a Balanced Scorecard, we don't over-index on one specific

metric. Rather, we make smart tradeoffs to optimize for the complex overall Uber ecosystem.

- **Set the right goals:** Sounds easy, but it's not. Goals need to be aggressive enough to push the team forward. But not so aggressive that the team gives up when the goals feel out of reach. And you want to avoid big negative surprises that could create material risks to plans or budgets. Goal setting is an art form that you'll get better at with practice. In Community Operations, I've fine-tuned my radar to identify *just the right amount of complaining* that I need to hear from each leader about a proposed goal so that I'm confident it is pushing folks out of their comfort zones, but not so much that the goal is likely unrealistic. Set goals so that your success rate is about 70% over time.
- **Ensure alignment:** If every reindeer has a different idea about the delivery route, Santa is in for a rough night. The same is true with your team. It's not enough to just have a plan. You also need to invest time in ensuring your plan is well understood by all of your stakeholders. You need a plan that is aligned from top to bottom. Operations is a team sport.
- **Know the <u>RAPID</u>:** It's important that team members know their role. Who's responsible for doing what, deciding what and approving what? This clarity helps with both the speed and quality of decision-making. At the North Pole, the elves are **R**esponsible for making the toys. The kids have **I**nput into the lists they submit. Parents must **A**gree to what gets submitted. Santa ultimately

Decides. Imagine the chaos (and tears) that would ensue without such clarity.

- **Drive structure and cadence:** Programmatic rigor is not the cool, sexy part of operations, but it is perhaps the most important driver of success. Good operators make complexity seem simple. Don't let the sense of monotony fool you. Operational discipline is the lifeblood of consistent and predictable execution. Define your cadence of 1:1s, operating reviews and initiative deep dives. Stick to them. Build them into your team's core operating model.
- **Practice The Five Whys:** A good operator asks lots of questions, regardless of whether things are going well or poorly. Your goal should be to get to the root cause of what drives outcomes. That means probing deeper and deeper until you truly understand what the underlying issue is and what needs to be done about it.
- **Sweat the details (selectively):** There's a reason why Santa not only makes a list, but also checks it twice. Mistakes are costly. And in Santa's case, mistakes lead to tears. A good operator knows enough about the underlying operations so that she can truly engage with and coach her team. Don't try to know every item on the list, but do know enough to be able to spot irregularities, identify opportunities and ask good questions.
- **Have some fun with it:** Operations is serious and sometimes grueling work. But nobody wants to work with The Grinch. It's okay to have some laughs and good times along the way. Santa is a stern taskmaster, but there's a

reason why they call him Jolly Saint Nick. The guy has the charisma, good cheer and jovial attitude that make the team want to put in the hard work needed to get the job done.

Whether you believe in Santa or not, I hope you can find inspiration in his skills and track record as an operator. And perhaps leave out some milk and cookies for him next year just in case.

DON'T STRESS IT

Uber's recent employee survey results revealed that many employees were feeling stressed. This result was evident across regions, levels and roles.

The challenge of managing employee stress and burn-out is not unique to Uber, and it's common across fast-growing and dynamic companies. Uber is growing at breakneck speed and facing fearsome competitors. And in Community Operations, we run 24 x 7 x 365 in every country of the world. We're the public face and voice of Uber. If we mess up, customers suffer. And we have almost a million opportunities every day to mess up. I'm getting stressed just thinking about it!

The right amount of stress (or eustress) is good. It motivates. It drives action. It teaches. One of the things I loved about coaching sports is the eustress of a close game against a tough opponent. I loved seeing a young pitcher walk to the mound when the game's on the line with a brave smile, but a tremble in his step and get it done. Or a shortstop making a game-losing error and quickly learning the life lesson that his teammates still love him, even if his coach grimaces a little. Stress is part of life.

But too much stress is a bad thing. It can have a negative impact on your work, and more important, your happiness and well being. It can create a vicious cycle where stress begets more stress. It leads to burnout and attrition.

You can't eliminate stress, but you can get better at reducing and managing it.

Here are some tactics that work for me:

Reducing Stress:

- When I feel overwhelmed, I make a list of everything I need to do. The list might look daunting, but at least I know I have visibility into what needs to get done. The simple act of writing it down is an immediate stress reducer because it removes two big root causes of stress: ambiguity and uncertainty.
- Next, I pick a couple of things on my list to actually get done. I don't pick based on what's most important or urgent. Rather, I pick things that I know I can get done quickly. Why? Because the act of physically crossing something off my list creates a sense of accomplishment and alleviates my anxiety.
- Next comes ruthless prioritization. I decide what's most critical or most pressing on my list and what can be deferred or skipped. I try to put a disproportionate share of my focus on the subset of things that are most critical.
- Sometimes it helps to talk to your manager or stakeholder. Let her know what you're stressed about and ask her what is most important for you to accomplish. More

often than not, you'll find that being open and transparent will enable conversations that reduce your stress.

Coping with Stress:

- The most important thing you can do to reduce stress is maintain a healthy balance in your life. You need to set boundaries, maintain your life outside of work, and get plenty of sleep and enough exercise.
- When you feel the most stressed, take a mental pause and try to put things in perspective. What's the worst that can happen? Is it as bad as you've convinced yourself it could be? Probably not. We all fail sometimes and we survive. I've coached kids who put so much pressure on themselves that they actually impair their performance. They forget it's just a game. Sometimes you're the hero and sometimes you're the goat. Life goes on. The vast majority of mistakes employees make are "survivable events." Sometimes they're even learning opportunities. Chill!
- It is okay to ask for help. If you work at a company like Uber, you have teammates who are there for you. You have a manager who has a vested interest in your success. Your company probably offers resources to help you manage stress, including a confidential Employee Assistance Program. There is no shame in asking for help. As a manager, I would rather have employees talk to me about how I can help them manage their stress than have them tell me they're leaving Uber because of the stress.

As a leader, you have a duty to your teammates and peers to help them manage their stress. And if you want to play on a winning team, you can't focus only on yourself.

Here's some things to think about:

- Be a leader who dampens stress for your team, not one who amplifies it. When you're feeling pressure from your manager, be a shock absorber. Push up, don't punch down.
- Coach your team about prioritization, balance and perspective. Don't do this just because it's the nice thing to do. Do it because it is in your best interest. Too much stress hinders innovation, slams productivity and fractures team chemistry. You'll get more out of your team when you reduce their stress.
- Be on the lookout for signs of your teammates' stress. When you sense something might be wrong, ask. Create room for honest dialogue. When you sense someone is nearing burnout, load balance or re-prioritize.
- Make time for fun and socialization with your team, especially when things are the busiest or most tense. That's when your team needs it most.

I'll close by quoting basketball legend Kareem Abdul-Jabar, "You have to be able to center yourself, to let all of your emotions go. Don't forget that you play with your soul as well as your body."

THE ART & SCIENCE OF DECISION MAKING

Leaders have to make a lot of decisions. But the process of decision-making is something we often take for granted. And given the importance of it, ignoring it is a bad decision.

Life would be so much easier if every time you had to make an important decision, you were fully aware of all the relevant information, options and ultimate results. You'd have less anxiety and seldom get the decision wrong. Your boss would come to see you as an infallible genius. It would be awesome at least until the AI robot overlords took over because in a world of perfect certainty, human decision-making would become obsolete.

So it's lucky for us humans that we live in a world rife with uncertainty and nuance. As a leader, you're going to have to make a lot of important decisions with incomplete facts, imperfect data and conflicting opinions from your stakeholders.

The first question to ask yourself is if you need to make a decision at all. Sometimes deferring a decision is actually a great decision. It enables you to collect more information and it preserves option value (i.e. flexibility.) But beware! Are you strategically deferring the decision or are you just avoiding it? By not making a decision, you're actually making a decision to stick with the status quo. Ironically, *non-decisions* are the most common decisions managers tend to make. Often they result in bad outcomes.

My first action when I'm confronted with a critical decision is to get more information. That usually means collecting more data or getting more perspectives from peers or teammates. It might mean building a model or doing some research. The hard reality is that the best way to make good decisions about complex or high-stakes topics is to put in the effort to be well informed. Sorry, there are no short-cuts.

But I do have some tips:

- **Playing the Odds:** I'm a big fan of Bayesian Logic as the best mental model to guide decision-making. Bayesian Logic is essentially a structured way to use probability-weighted outcomes to arrive at the decision with the highest expected positive benefit. It is a fun topic worth exploring (i.e., Google it). It will also help your poker game.
- ***No Regrets* Decisions:** Try to find ways to minimize the downside of being wrong and ensure the direction you take will provide benefits even if it turns out not to be the best long-term direction.
- **Staging:** Look for opportunities to divide a big decision into a series of smaller decisions over time so you can learn along the way and course-correct as needed. Don't

"over-decide" everything upfront. Decide just enough to get the ball rolling.

- **Course-correcting:** Once a decision has been made, don't put the topic aside. Stay close to the situation and watch how it unfolds. Look for opportunities to finetune or even unwind the decision, if it's not panning out as you wanted. Keep an open mind.

It's also important to avoid pitfalls in evaluating the quality of decisions once they have played out. We live in a world with lots of externalities and moving parts. Sample sizes are small. Just because a bet doesn't work out doesn't mean it was the wrong decision to place it. Looking only at the quantitative outcomes of past decisions can be misleading. Try to evaluate the quality of a decision not by the outcomes alone, but also by the logic and rationale you used to arrive at it.

Let me tell you a little secret. Sometimes the actual decision you make is less important than the process you use to arrive at that decision. A *good-enough* decision that is enthusiastically embraced and well executed by your team will probably yield better results than a *perfect* decision that your team doesn't support or isn't prepared to execute. As a leader, it is important that you make key stakeholders feel like they have input into the process and are excited about the plan. Not only will that create the right conditions for your decision to be well-executed, it will also yield better decisions.

I hope you now feel more confident about making your next big decision. But if not, you can always flip a coin and be right half the time!

DEALING WITH 'BAD CALLS'

(AND WORKING THE REFS A BIT)

One of the more interesting things about coaching kids is that your games are officiated by youth referees instead of experienced professional officials. And although the young refs work hard and usually do a great job, you get your share of bad calls that can have a big impact on the game.

I try to keep it (somewhat) hidden, but I'm a pretty competitive person. I have to tone this competitive fire down when it comes to coaching kids, especially after a blown call turns a hard-fought win into a painful loss. My natural inclination is to charge onto the field to argue. Then I remind myself that: The ref is fourteen years old. His mom is probably watching from the bleachers and she's probably super proud that her son had the courage to sign up for such a hard job. Most of the parents have smartphones and I don't want to end up a viral sensation on YouTube. And I'm supposed to be teaching my kiddos not just sports skills, but also sportsmanship. But it's hard!

Here's how I deal with a bad call:

- I remind myself that the refs are doing their best to make good decisions, often in a very stressful environment.

And that I certainly make my share of bad calls as a coach.

- I consider the possibility that what I think was a bad call was actually the right call. After all, the ref has a much better vantage point on the field than I have on the sideline. Maybe my daughter really was offsides, even though it didn't look like it from my angle.
- I comfort myself with the thought that bad calls will even out over time. Sometimes they'll go in my favor. Sometimes they won't. The mistakes will be evenly distributed and probably won't impact the season one way or the other.
- I face the hard truth that arguing a bad call might not work in my favor. In addition to making me look like a jerk in front of the other parents, berating the ref may mean that more future calls will also go against me. Maybe I'll even get ejected and cost my team the game.

That said, I do have a right to ask the ref why she made the decision she did and maybe to delicately make my case. After all, I want to ensure that I understand the rules, represent my team well and maybe strategically guide the refs toward future decisions that will be favorable for my team. But I do this sparingly, carefully and thoughtfully.

At work, sometimes the ref is your manager, your business partner or your colleague. And sometimes these people make calls you don't agree with. Sometimes the calls have a real impact on the direction of a project you're passionate about or the outcome of a promotion. Just like in sports, business people make bad calls. Or at least, what you might think was a bad call. Believe it or not, sometimes you'll even make bad calls as a leader.

My suggestion is that when you feel you've been impacted by a bad call:

- Ask yourself if it really was a bad call. Do you have all the information about why the decision was made? Are you letting your self-interest color your reaction? Is it possible that it might be the right call? Most of the time, your best move is to put the bad call behind you and focus on what you can do to get a better call the next time.
- If you're still not satisfied, ask the decision-maker for additional context and perspective about the decision. But do it in a mature and non accusatory way.
- Explain your perspective to the decision-maker. It's okay to work the refs a little. You're probably not going to reverse a call that has already been made, but perhaps you'll influence the next one. How do you do that effectively?
    - Depersonalize the conversation. Don't make it about yourself. Make it about the process, rationale and facts.
    - Be respectful. Let the decision-maker know that you understand that making hard decisions is challenging and not everyone will agree.
    - Focus on understanding the reason for the decision, not arguing the outcome.
    - Get over it and move on. Focus on the future instead of reliving the past.

Bad calls are a part of life. You don't have to like them, but you do need to be prepared to deal with them. Be careful not to make matters worse by handling them poorly. Over time, you'll get some bad calls in your favor, too. I promise.

THE INTANGIBLES

One of the tough lessons I learned through coaching youth basketball is that innate talent and physical advantages are not evenly distributed. Rather, there are wide variations in the size and coordination of kids on a team. Early in the season, the bigger, stronger and more athletic kids dominate. As Utah Jazz basketball coach Frank Layden said, "You can't coach your players how to be taller."

By the end of the season, things have changed. "The naturals" are still generally playing many of the key positions. But other kids are also logging a lot of court time. Even though they aren't as big or as fast, they're making critical contributions. How do these less-gifted athletes achieve this?

Intangibles matter! What these kids have is typically a mix of:

- **Hard work:** They're the first to arrive at practice and the last to leave. They identify areas in which they want to improve and they put in tremendous effort to do so.

- **Teamwork:** They know how to pass the ball. They know how to make the critical assists. They know how to make those around them better players.
- **Hustle:** They dive for every loose ball. They never quit on a play. They put the maximum effort into everything they do.
- **Flexibility:** They learn how to play multiple positions, which makes it easier for the coach to plug them into different roles based on the team's evolving needs.
- **Attitude:** They're a joy to coach because they're positive, uplifting and enthusiastic. Good attitudes are contagious. They make the team dynamic stronger.
- **Respectful:** They show up on time, every time. They don't whine or complain. They treat the coaches and officials and their competitors with respect.

In my son's favorite movie, *Thunderstruck*, Kevin Durant's key line is "hard work beats talent when talent fails to work hard." But that's not directly relevant here, as KD has unbelievable physical gifts and a legendary work ethic. That's unstoppable. So perhaps a better example is one of my favorite players, Muggsy Bogues. Muggsy played fourteen seasons in the NBA, scoring almost 7,000 points. At 5'3", he's the shortest player in NBA history. In one of the most famous plays in basketball history, he blocked a shot taken by 7' hall-of-famer, Patrick Ewing. Muggsy was all heart, hustle and teamwork. He made those around him better. When he retired, he went on to coach high school basketball. Vertically challenged and a youth coach... you can see why I admire him so much!

Like in sports, there are a variety of skills that are important to success and progression in the workplace. These skills may differ by role, but the list often includes things like analytical ability, presentation skills, problem-solving prowess, charisma and business acumen. Although there are some "naturals" among us, for whom everything seems to flow effortlessly, for most of us that's not the case. The intangibles matter. And if you go back through the list of attributes I highlighted about basketball, I think you'll find each one also strongly correlates with professional success. What a coincidence!

Finally, here's a fact most coaches won't admit. We probably tend to give the kids who focus on the intangibles more coaching and more playing time than they deserve based on their raw talent. So if you're not a natural, don't let your limitations limit you. Offset them by focusing on attributes that are within your control. Be like Muggsy.

HOW TO GO FASTER

Speed. Perhaps no trait has been more essential to the survival of the human race. In ancient times, *speed* determined if you would eat dinner or be dinner. The very first sporting event was probably two villagers racing each other to the riverbank and back. Even today, the winner of the Olympics 100-meter race instantly becomes one of the world's most celebrated athletes. Speed matters!

Speed has driven Uber's success. We got here (and there, and everywhere) first. We scaled faster. We innovated quicker. It was our secret sauce. But let's be honest—probably not so much anymore. The need to "execute faster" has been a theme leadership has been emphasizing, and perhaps something you've found frustrating in your day to day work. We need to recapture our speed, without cutting corners.

I learned about *speed* while serving as the sprints-and-jumps coach for my kids' track team. I loved it. There are few sports you can coach in which you're able to drive such tangible and measurable results. The clock doesn't lie. The feedback and improvement loop is immediate.

I took the job knowing little about track-and-field. Over the course of the season, and with the help of YouTube, here's what I learned about running fast:

- The start matters a lot. When the gun sounds, you need to be first out of the blocks. The runner who leads after the first few seconds often wins the race.
- Running fast requires intense focus. Top sprinters figure out how to shed all distractions and focus intently on their running form.
- It's important to have a training plan and stick to it, even if you don't get faster every day. Trust the plan and avoid the temptation to tweak it based on anecdotes.
- Run hard all the way through the finish line. Don't let up just because you're getting close.
- Be aware of your competitors. But if you break form staring at them, they will pass you. Run your own race.

I also had an interesting insight from sprint relays: adding more people to the team can actually slow the team down. In a 4 x 100 relay (i.e., one lap around the track), a team of four 100-meter sprinters should beat a single 400-meter runner. But a team of eight runners would lose not only to the team of four, but even to a single sprinter. That's because the additional handoffs and coordination required to make the extra baton passes more than offset the added horsepower of more runners.

Here are my thoughts about how teams can move faster in a business environment:

- Small teams are more agile than big teams. Don't add more people than you need to get the work done.
- Make sure your project or function has clearly defined roles and responsibilities. Who gets to have input? Who gets to decide? Sometimes the best thing you can do is to butt out to avoid slowing down your peers or your team. Trust them.
- Don't let disagreement or confusion linger. Solve it in the room. Failing to do so often means another meeting and another few days or weeks of inaction. Disagree and commit.
- Streamline your calendar, and start saying "no" to meetings in which you are unlikely to benefit or add substantial value. Create more time to do the work that matters most. If you're the meeting organizer, be thoughtful about inviting only the people you need.
- Don't overthink things. Make decisions quickly, especially when you're confronted with decisions that can be course-corrected over time.
- Don't let perfect be the enemy of *good enough*. If it's worth doing, it's worth doing poorly. You can improve it later.
- Work harder. The person, team or company that puts in the greatest effort usually wins whether it's in sports, business or any other endeavor. There are no "participation trophies" in a dog-eat-dog industry.

A final caution: Don't run so fast that you lose sight of where you're going. You can end up running in the wrong direction. Sometimes speed can even get you into trouble if it causes you to sacrifice good judgment or moral clarity. The goal is sustained and controlled speed of execution, not a reckless dash. Ready, set, go!

LEADING WITH HUMILITY

Make a list of traits you think are most associated with leadership success (I'll wait).

My guess is that *humility* didn't make your list. After all, it's not often associated with icons like Steve Jobs, Elon Musk or Jeff Bezos. And for those who possess their unique blend of brilliance and magnetism, it probably wouldn't be the optimal approach. But for the rest of us, humility can play a critical role in our success and our teams' success.

The irony of career progression is that with every step you take up the ladder, the less you know about the core elements of your job. The broader your scope, the less you're able to rely on your own expertise and skills and the more reliant you become on the capabilities of the people you work with. You might think that moving into bigger jobs would make one more arrogant—and for some people it clearly does—but I think it should actually make leaders more humble.

I'm surrounded by people who know a lot more about the specifics of what they do than I could ever hope to learn. Sometimes that can be intimidating.

Regardless of your current career stage or job, humility is a virtue that will serve you well. There is no magic recipe for how to lead with humility, but here are some tips:

- Focus more on asking others good questions instead of always trying to figure out the best answers yourself. The best way to scale your impact is by stimulating the thinking and contributions of all the smart and capable people with whom you work.
- Recognize that the most important factor in your success is surrounding yourself with the right team. The best teams have a diversity of experience, expertise and thinking styles. Such teams approach tough challenges in balanced, holistic and multi-faceted ways.
- Be careful not to block too much light. Give others a chance to shine. It's the only way you'll keep talented peers and team members engaged and contributing. Recognize that a leader's accolades are driven mainly by what their team achieves, not their individual contributions to those results.
- Identify, admit and learn from your mistakes. There will be many, and you'll learn more from them than from all your successes combined.
- Share more about yourself and your insecurities than you might feel comfortable sharing. Don't do this with everyone you work with, but find a core group of folks with whom you feel comfortable enough to do so. If you don't let yourself be at least a little vulnerable at times,

you won't reap the benefits of feedback, mentoring and coaching.

- Be genuine. You might be able to "fake it" for a while, but that won't serve you well in the long term. Disingenuousness eventually fails because people won't trust your motives. Plus, putting on an act all the time would be exhausting.
- Find the right balance between being *unsure* and being *confident*. A leader needs to reflect a certain amount of confidence to inspire and influence others, but also display enough humility to invite colleagues, particularly those more junior, to advocate for their ideas and challenge their own.

Having humility doesn't mean you lack authority, energy or personal insight. That would be a recipe for disaster. And there will be times when a particular challenge or situation requires you to be a more dictatorial leader. The power trip of doing so can be an adrenaline rush. Don't let it become a bad habit.

Imagine you're a professional baseball coach. The batters are better hitters than you are. The defenders are better fielders than you are. All of your players are younger, faster and stronger than you are. But you're the one who's in charge. You won't be successful by trying to do your players' jobs better than they do them. And your team will self-destruct if your stars feel like you're taking all the credit and basking in the limelight.

Rather, the best thing you can do is build the right team, put your players in positions to succeed, have a good game plan and make sure your team knows that you value their contributions and you *have their backs*. And if you're managing a team of second graders, bring plenty of snacks and juice boxes.

GIVING AND RECEIVING FEEDBACK

Feedback is a gift, though it might not always feel that way while you're receiving it. But hearing candid and actionable feedback is the best way to learn about your strengths and areas in need of development, as well as how others perceive you. In the workplace, perception is often reality. In the eyes of others, you are your reputation, whether you think it's legit or not. You do yourself a disservice when you don't solicit feedback regularly and you're derelict as a manager when you don't share feedback just as often.

But feedback is hard. It can be uncomfortable to give, not to mention to get. As a result, it often ends up on the "I'll get around to it later, but never actually do it" list. Let's see if we can break down some of those barriers by understanding how to give and receive feedback in a better way.

Tips for Giving Feedback:

- Schedule it or it won't happen. Don't wait for performance review cycles or surveys. Make it a part of your regular management process.

- Be balanced. Don't jump straight to what someone else is doing wrong. It's not about being *nice;* it's about being effective. Serve a *feedback sandwich* that starts with a positive, then layers in a development area and then closes with positive encouragement. I aim for a 2:1 ratio of positive feedback to constructive feedback. It tastes better.
- Make feedback as specific and actionable as possible. Not only does that make it more understandable, but it also gives the recipient an improvement path to focus on.
- Make it clear that you're proving the feedback from a place of good intentions. You're doing it because you legitimately care and you're rooting for the recipient's success.
- Allow the recipient time to reflect. Don't turn the conversation into a debate or start barking out action items. Follow up a few days later to start turning feedback into plans.
- Ask for upward feedback as part of the process.

Tips for **Receiving** Feedback:

- Ask and you shall receive. It's not easy for employees to give feedback to their boss, so you need to actively draw it out by making it clear that you genuinely want to hear it.
- Don't ask *just* your boss for feedback. In fact, that might be the least helpful feedback you get since she has to be more careful about what she shares. Expand your personal board of directors to include peers and partners. You'll get much more candid and diverse feedback from them.

- Avoid being defensive about what you hear, even if it's *wrong*. Remember, perception is sometimes reality. So accept feedback as legit. But pick and choose what you want to act on and what you don't. Don't try to tackle everything immediately.
- Develop a clear and actionable personal development plan, using feedback as a component. Make your plan as robust and rigorous as you would a plan for your most important business deliverable. Because it is!

Some of my most valuable mentor relationships came about as a direct result of asking for feedback. In addition to gaining insights, the process of asking for feedback can turn your detractors into mentors. Why? Because it is flattering when someone respects you enough to value and ask for your feedback. And it creates some earnest vulnerability, which helps to develop deeper relationships. So my feedback to each of you: don't underestimate the importance of giving and receiving feedback to your effectiveness as a leader.

CUSTOMER OBSESSION

I'm hearing a lot about **#CustomerObsession** lately. I love it! Giving teams a sense of purpose is essential to driving higher engagement and better results. However, the challenge with customer obsession is that it's an easy value to talk about, but a hard one to actualize.

There are three key levers that are critical to driving greater customer obsession:

Role model customer-obsession

- You have to dig into actual customer support interactions. Every month. You have to hang with customers in the physical world. Frequently. You can't lead people-who-serve-customers if you do not have a visceral sense of the challenges they encounter, the tools they use and the emotions they feel. It is the only way to have credibility as a leader. It is the only way to hone your instincts. Get in the game!
- Don't tolerate mediocrity. Don't sweep things under the rug. Be a pain in the ass when you see something that just

isn't right from a customer experience perspective.

- Celebrate when someone does something awesome for the customer experience even when it can't be quantified. Especially then, actually. Do it publicly, loudly and repeatedly. Make sure your team sees what you value. Make storytelling part of your leadership repertoire.

Set expectations with your teams and reinforce them in every interaction

- Start team meetings by asking: "What are you hearing from customers lately and what are we doing as a result?" Do this for long enough, and your teams will learn to always show up prepared to have an in-depth discussion about customer sentiment and feedback.
- Be clear that you expect customer obsession in every meeting. When someone shares a proposal or slide-deck with you, probe to ensure they have truly thought about the end-to-end customer experience and not just the near-term financial impact. If you're not satisfied, tell them to start over. You'll be amazed at how sending a team back to the drawing board changes future presentations.

Ensure team buy-in and understanding

- Ensure that you and your team are active customers not merely to better understand customers' pain points, but also to develop empathy and intuition about customers.
- Ensure that every employee has a customer-focused goal that he or she can personally impact. These goals help

employees feel more personally connected to the goal of customer loyalty.

- Make customer immersion a core part of onboarding new hires. Have them spend a week serving customers as a way to learn and because of the message it sends to the team about what you value.

Most of us are accustomed to living in a world of facts and data. And the ideas above will be hard to analyze. It requires taking it on faith that focusing on creating a more customer-obsessed culture will drive tangible business success. But if you look at any loyalty-leading company, you'll find that they put tremendous focus on topics related to culture, behaviors and values. There are no shortcuts if you want to become one of them.

FINDING BALANCE

I'm not going to be pollyannaish. Being a leader is hard. The demands are high. The hours can be long. The pressure intense. That's what we signed up for. It's super exciting, but also daunting. So get ready for a marathon, not a sprint. And the first rule for marathons is not to burn yourself out in the first mile.

You're not doing yourself, your team or your company any favors if you push yourself so hard that you sacrifice cognitive acuity, mental creativity or emotional positivity. Your team and your company need the best you, not a constantly exhausted and drained you.

So you've got to make work-life balance, or integration, an important thing.

Let's start by busting some urban legends:

- The myth that you can't take vacations is a myth. You *can* and you *should*. I do.

- Facetime is an app, not a thing. You don't have to stay in the office just so people can see you in the office.
- Nobody cares how hard you work. They care about how much impact you have.

There is no one-size-fits-all answer to balance. We all have different priorities, are at different life stages and do different jobs. So I can't give you the one and only *answer.* I can only tell you it is important that you actively think about what the *best answer is for you.*

Here's what works for me:

- I prioritize relentlessly and over-index on the things that either have the biggest potential for impact or where I think I can personally add the most value.
- I obsess about seconds and hate waste. I strive for a high return on investment for every minute I spend on work.
- I'm flexible and I integrate work with life. Sometimes that means coaching my son's soccer team Friday afternoon and then writing emails on Sunday morning.
- I use technology as an enabler, not an addiction. Yes, you'll catch me peeking at my smartphone at all hours. But doing so is enabling me to not constantly be at my desk.
- I set boundaries. That means not missing school conferences and weekend bike rides.
- I recognize that there will be weeks when I'll have to put in long hours to accomplish something important, but I

recognize that if those weeks start to pile up, I'm doing something wrong and I need to step back and figure out how to address it.

That's what works for me. I encourage you to find what works for you and make it happen. As managers, we need to remember that being honest and human with our direct reports about workloads, boundaries and priorities is a great way to engage and motivate our teams.

Now get back to work!

ANALOGISTIC LEARNING

In a futile attempt to avert a midlife crisis, last year I fulfilled a long time ambition to experience driving a fast car very fast (legally). After signing a very long waiver, I found myself behind the wheel of a beautiful red Ferrari on the road course at the Las Vegas Motor Speedway.

I'm not really a "*car guy*" and this was my first time on a racetrack. After the proverbial checkered flag fell, the rest was a blur of revving engines, screeching tires and sweating hands. But upon reflection, I actually learned some interesting lessons about racing that can apply much more broadly:

- **Direction:** For my first couple of turns, I tried to hug the inside rail as tightly as possible, figuring that the shorter the distance driven, the faster the time. Turns out, trying to cut corners actually slows you down. You get a much faster time by planning your lines into each curve and maintaining your speed as long as possible. The fastest time between two points isn't necessarily the shortest route.

- **Focus:** I can't remember the last time I was so fully aware and truly in the moment. In a race car, there's no time for daydreaming and certainly no time for multi-tasking! This focus translates into heightened performance and more enjoyment of the experience. Eliminating distractions and truly focusing on the task is a key ingredient for success.
- **Coaching:** A primary reason I survived and enjoyed the experience was that I had a professional driver by my side throughout. He educated me about the car, taught me racing techniques, shared his wisdom and made me feel safe. All this without ever taking the wheel. When you're learning new things, there is no substitute for having a great mentor and coach.
- **Intensity:** One of the first things the professional driver taught me about the road course was that you are always either fully on the throttle (accelerating out of the turn onto the straights) or fully on the brake (going into the curves). There is no coasting or half measures if you want to post a fast lap.
- **Competition:** Given the intensity of the experience, I was laser-focused on the track and the cars in front of me. And then suddenly seemingly from out of nowhere, another driver passed me. If you aren't aware of what your competitors, including those who are well behind you, are doing , you're at risk of getting overtaken when you least expect it.

Next year, maybe skydiving. My bucket-list is still quite long!

MANAGING UP

In previous Coach's Corners, I've shared thoughts on being a better people manager. But each of us also has a manager of our own. So it's important to understand how you can also be a better managee.

When I was starting my career as a management consultant, my goal was to involve my manager as little as possible. After all, what better way was there for me to demonstrate my value and self-sufficiency, right? Wrong. During an unpleasant performance review, the wise senior partner told me that by cutting her out of the loop, I'd made it difficult for her to add value, provide guidance and feel connected to the client. And I'd cheated myself out of her ability to coach me. So an early lesson I learned was that my definition of success should not be *how low-maintenance I could be for my boss.*

The term "managing up" gets a bad rap. But I don't think it should. It is not about kissing butts or flattery. It is about becoming someone who is easy to manage and can be managed effectively, benefiting both parties.

So how do you do this? The answer depends on what your manager is looking for, but here are some tips I've found universally applicable:

- **Be organized:** Come to one-on-one meetings prepared and structured. Have a clear plan for what you want to cover and what feedback you need. It's fine to allow some time just to gab, but make it clear that you value your manager's time enough to not just wing it.

  Send regular emails about key topics or issues your manager should be aware of. Be succinct and make it super clear whether you're informing your manager or asking for input.

- **Ask for help:** Find a few topics on which to really go deep with your manager. Jam a bit. You'll gain insights into how she thinks about the problem. You'll build relationships. You'll make him feel valued. And who knows? You might even learn something.

  Personally, I'd rather be over-copied and over-included. It is easier for me to pick and choose which topics to engage in than it is for me to not know what I don't know. But every manager is different, so my advice is to ask yours how much detail she prefers rather than to just guess.

- **Surface problems, challenges and risks early and clearly:** Most managers understand that problems and failures are part of life. We've all been there. But surprises…that's another thing. It's always better to be transparent and forthright. It builds trust.

- **Leverage strengths and augment weaknesses:** Figure out what your manager is really good at and try to use that to help advance the team's goals. Maybe you'll even learn a bit from her along the way.

  Figure out what your manager is bad at. Keep in mind that your manager might not actually know what that is. Self-awareness is not universal human strength. Find ways to augment his weaknesses to avoid derailing the team's goals.

- **Give constructive upward feedback:** The more senior you become in an organization, the less feedback you get. Which is unfortunate, because the more senior you become, the more feedback you probably need.

  Tread lightly at first, but if you sense the door is open for honest and direct upward feedback, inch your way in.

HAPPY TEAMMATES → HAPPY CUSTOMERS

I'm a self-confessed metrics geek. So one of the cool parts of leading an operational function like Community Operations is that we are awash in so much wonderful data, statistics and trend-lines. It's nerd heaven!

I don't (usually) play favorites with my kids, but I do with my metrics. And there's one metric that is, hands down, the most important for Community Operations… and it's probably not the one you think.

Drum roll, please. That metric is **eNPS** (i.e., employee engagement), particularly with regard to our front-line agents, experts and leads. Here's why:

- Our agents and experts have millions of interactions with customers.
- Each of these interactions makes an indelible impression on a customer and thereby shapes the Uber brand for better or worse.
- Engaged and enthusiastic employees exude these same emotions to our customers. The opposite applies as well.

It's not rocket science.

- Likewise, high eNPS support organizations have less attrition, better quality and higher productivity. The holiday parties are more fun, too!

How do I know all of this? With some trepidation, I'll share a personal story...

Several years ago, in a different company, I received one of the worst eNPS scores within my organization. After getting my results, I was afraid of the implications in terms of my career. But days passed, and my manager never even mentioned it to me. It turned out that leadership didn't seem to care about our eNPS since my team was hitting our numbers. So why should I worry about eNPS?

I pushed it out of my mind for a week or so, but stewed about it over the following weekend. If my team was feeling disengaged, was this impacting our performance metrics? How was this disengagement being felt by our customers? And what did it say about me as a leader? As I played out the likely answers to these questions in my mind, I didn't like the results.

So I committed to improving eNPS. The only problem was that I had absolutely no idea how to do so. That's when the *metrics geek* in me came to the rescue. Perhaps improving employee engagement was no different than improving any other metric. So here's what we did:

- **Listened:** We read lots of feedback reports verbatim and did several focus groups and interviews. We dug into the data. The key drivers of discontent soon became clear. And they weren't the ones I would have guessed.

- **Planned:** We took what we learned and created a robust, detailed and actionable improvement plan just like we would for any other critical initiative. We needed clarity and accountability to drive action.

- **Prioritized:** We made eNPS a priority. We made tough decisions about where to focus our resources. We were relentless about emphasizing the importance up and down the organization. We made it clear to managers that eNPS was not a secondary consideration.

- **Involved:** We shared our data, benchmarks, plans and goals with the whole organization. More importantly, we enlisted the help of dozens of people at all levels of the division to help drive improvement.

- **Celebrated:** We started recognizing and celebrating our best people managers and culture carriers. We held them up as the heroes they truly were.

A year later, the eNPS results arrived. With bated breath, I clicked the link in the email to learn if our months of effort had born fruit. But then, a calm washed over me because I realized I knew the answer before I even looked at the results. I knew because the organization just felt different now. Little by little, we changed the culture, the dynamic and the vibe. And it was equally clear that this change translated into better business and customer outcomes. Personally, I was having more fun coming to work every day. And I liked it!

Finally, I reminded my team they were the collective management team of a critical function, and one that has an enormous day-to-day impact on how millions of customers feel about our company. For us to be successful, every team member needs to obsess about creating a positive and engaging environment for the *thousands of agents* that they collectively lead and enable. And for themselves as well.

ALWAYS BE LEARNING

Former eBay CEO John Donahoe was once asked at a company leadership offsite what he considered to be his key strength. I assumed he'd say leadership, courage, relationship building or strategic insight. But his answer was quite different. He said it was his ability to learn from absolutely anybody and his obsession about doing so. In all his interactions, he said, he focused more on what he could absorb than what he could impart.

I realize in retrospect how obvious his answer was. How can any individual have the broad array of expertise and experience necessary to lead a massive, diverse, complex and far-flung enterprise? Only by opening ourselves up to the vast expertise and experiences of those around us, can we lever our own capabilities many times over.

Today I lead a function that is mission-critical to one of the world's most important companies. Confidentially, between you and me, it is terrifying and I sometimes feel woefully unprepared! No amount of personal experience could have prepared me for this job. So my approach has been to take Donahoe's advice about learning from everybody and *borrowing* as many good ideas as I can.

Here are partial list of some examples of people I've tried to learn from and emulate in approaching my job:

- Bruce (My first boss—the salesman): Strived to deeply understand the motivations, biases and needs of others and in doing so, made the actual selling part easy.
- Steve (My boss at eBay): If you get the KPIs, goals, cadences and organizational stuff right, business results will fall into place. But there is nothing more important than building a culture of engaged front-line teammates.
- Wendy (My boss at Schwab): You can be an incredibly nice and caring person while also setting a high bar and pushing people to do great things.
- Amanda (Uber Customer Service Rep): "Sometimes there's no substitute for talking to the customer. It drives me crazy when we can't just pick up the phone and call."
- Chuck (Schwab founder): There are times when you have to ignore the spreadsheets and make decisions based on core values. But be careful, because the math is usually right.
- Katrina (BCG partner): Figure out where you can add value and dig in deep. Delegate the rest to people who know more than you.
- Dara (Uber CEO): Be cool, calm and collected during a crisis and set a clear plan for how to emerge from it stronger.

- Travis (Uber founder): Sometimes you have to be hard on people to help them learn what they are capable of accomplishing.
- Juan (Uber Greenlight Hub expert): The best way to make a nervous new driver feel at ease is to give her tips you learned from when you started driving on the platform.
- Joanie (My mom): Adventure, fitness and fun are key ingredients to a happy and productive life. Turn off your friggin' phone sometimes.
- Buster (My dog): Letting your unbridled emotions shine through is a great way to build relationships even when you don't quite understand everything going on around you.

That's hardly a complete list and my favorite part about working with so many amazing people at Uber is that I get to add to the list every day.

Here's what I've learned about lifelong learning:

- Make learning a priority. Learn from everybody, not just your managers or those senior to you.
- Learn from the most diverse set of people possible. Make learning an active and conscious priority.
- If you're not learning something from everyone you regularly interact with, you're probably not paying close enough attention.
- You can learn a lot about the real world part of your company by spending time with front-line agents. They are

perhaps the most under-leveraged resources at many companies.

- Don't be afraid to copy. Imitation is the highest form of flattery.
- Keep track of what you learn. Make a list.

I hope you learn something from this book and that you'll put it to use to better yourself and your company. But remember, he who steals from me steals twice!

STARTING A NEW SEASON

A core element of coaching sports is that every season comes to end and then a new one begins. Over time, I've had some winning seasons and some losing seasons. Some all-star teams and some turnaround projects. A few championship banners and a lot of participation trophies. The changing of the seasons is part of both the fun and the challenge of being a coach.

There are a number of things I like to do as a sporting season ends and the team is gearing up for the next one. And many of the same principles apply at work as well.

I like to start each season by looking back and reflecting on how I felt about the past season in terms of the team's results and my impact as the coach. Some of the things I like to ponder include:

- First and foremost, the numbers. What was our win-loss record and where did we finish in the standings? Yeah, there is more to life than winning and losing, but I'm a competitive guy and we play to win. The scoreboard is there for a reason, and truth be told, participation trophies don't have a long shelf life in our house.

- But the final official standings only tell part of the story. The real value comes from deep-diving into the underlying reasons for our results. It's important to dig into factors that contributed to both the Ws and Ls. Sometimes it was just an (un)lucky bounce, and not worth obsessing over. But usually there are good learnings in terms of strategy, tactics and team performance that can provide actionable insight. So it's important to understand *the why*, not just *the what.*
- I think about the team roster. Who were the players that really stepped up and helped us win—and do I feel confident that they had a good experience so that they'll sign up again next season. Which players struggled, and what can I do as a coach to help them develop. And did I have some players that didn't even make an effort, or whose attitude brought the whole team down, and would the team be better off without them next season. I also think holistically about our lineup, and try to figure out some of the skill gaps that I want to fill.
- It's important to look beyond just my team, and try to understand what competitors in the league did, particularly those that turned in strong results. There are usually good things that can be learned (and copied), vulnerabilities that can be exploited and perhaps even some strong players that can be poached.

- Lastly, I do a hard assessment of myself as the coach. If I came into the season with a good gameplan, and if I was nimble in adapting it as reality unfolded. I ask myself if I helped put my team in a position to succeed, if I removed as many barriers as I could, if I developed my talent and fostered a strong team culture. But most importantly, if I created an environment in which the kids felt like they learned, thrived and had a lot of fun—because that is the key ingredient for them to want to play for me again next year.

We can learn a lot from the past, but we can't change it. So it's important not to spend too much time celebrating what's already happened or beating yourself about past mistakes. The most important part of the offseason is getting ready for the *next* season. Some things I like to do include:

- I think about our longer term vision and strategy, and how it might need to be adapted based on what we've learned and how the world is evolving. In most cases, it would be counterproductive to completely throw out the playbook and start from scratch. That's going to be too much change to throw at the team all at once, and probably an over-correction. Rather, success usually comes from adapting and fine tuning, while throwing in some exciting new plays to keep competitors on their heels.
- Do a pulse check with your team, peers and partners. Make sure you understand what they are hoping to achieve next season, and the key strategies and tactics they are deploying to do so. If every player on the team

has different objectives and approaches, the team is going to get off to a bumpy start.

- Have a plan. A goal without a plan is just a wish. Life is complicated, and I know things won't unfold exactly the way we expected, but the act of planning itself is invaluable. It prepares you for eventualities, sets a solid foundation for the team and helps drive alignment.
- Know your budget and make sure you are optimizing every dollar of it. In professional sports, that means making sure you're signing your top players (and prospects) to long term deals. In youth sports, it means that you understand the expenses of running the team and don't come up short for the season-ending pizza party. And in business, it means being thoughtful about where each dollar is best deployed.
- Finally, don't forget about **you**. The team needs you, and they need you to be at your best. So make sure you are taking the time to create a personal development plan that will truly challenge and guide your growth as a leader. And then discuss that plan with your mentors and manager.

Next Season is going to be here before you know it. In fact, it already is. So now is the perfect time to do some backwards-looking reflection and forwards-looking strategizing.

CAREER HACKS

There are no shortcuts to building a successful career, but there are "hacks" you can deploy to help grease the skids along the way. I'm going to share a few of my favorite career hacks. As is the case with any type of hack, proceed with caution. These have worked for me, but your mileage may vary.

- **Little things matter a lot**. Maybe not right away, but they add up over time. Make sure you're practicing good *professional hygiene*. That means showing up on time, responding to emails promptly, following through on your commitments, including the small ones, and being kind. You will be surprised how much ahead of the curve you'll be simply by nailing the fundamentals, since many people don't.
- **Find ways to be *useful* to your boss**. Consistently doing your job well is not usually a differentiator in high-performance cultures. Find ways to help with things she cares about, but aren't getting done well. Look

for ways to make his life easier. For example, maybe she hates writing slide decks, so you offer to take on more of that responsibility. Maybe he can't attend a big meeting, so you offer to cover and provide a summary. Whatever. Just be useful.

- **Own a metric or concrete deliverable**. Business is a team sport, but it's important to have some specific things you can point to that you directly impacted. This hack will also help you focus on how to tenaciously get things done and create some tangible proof-points you can reference. Plus, it is gratifying to watch a number move and know it was because of your actions.
- **Help colleagues, even when there is no upside for you in doing so.** A lot of stuff in life is transactional, including at work. That's not a bad thing, as it generally results in optimized and efficient outcomes. But what comes around goes around. Perhaps it's karma. Or perhaps people just remember others who have been helpful to them and find ways to return the favor.
- **You are always being evaluated**. Sorry, I don't mean to stress you out. But the reality is that your reputation is a synthesis of a lot of things. Every interaction, meeting or email contributes to it. Every presentation. Every question you ask. For better or for worse, you're always being evaluated by your manager, your peers and your team. So be cognizant and thoughtful about the reputation you want to build. Which brings me to...

- **...manage your *brand*.** Have a strategy and plan for what you want other people to think about you. Start by writing a few bullet points about what you want your personal brand to stand for. Make them compelling and at least somewhat unique. Have a personal brand management and marketing plan. Double down on the aspects you really want people to remember.
- In the words of Wayne Gretzky, **"Skate to where the puck is going, not to where it is."** Figure out what the next big thing is going to be and find a way to get involved with it. That doesn't mean changing your job every time a new priority emerges at work, but at least think about how you might shift your focus a bit. That's where the opportunities for impact and advancement will be and you want to at least be in the mix. You don't need to be Nostradamus to figure it out. Usually you just need to be paying attention.
- **Don't let your qualifications get in the way of applying for a role you think you can crush.** Job descriptions articulate what a perfect candidate would look like. But perfect candidates are rare. Don't worry if you can't check every box, just make sure you have a vision and passion for how you'd succeed in the role if you're selected.
- **Be great at *the how*.** Yes, you have to deliver on *the what*, but that's not enough. If people like working *with* you, they'll find ways to help you succeed. If people like working *for* you, they'll deliver for you. And the reverse is even

more true. Make sure that you act in a way that makes people want to root for you. You'll be surprised how much wind that puts at your back career-wise.

- **You can survive most things. But not all things.** You're going to have some bad days at work. You might have a big presentation to a senior leader that bombs. Or a bug in your model that you somehow missed. Most executives sit through presentation after presentation every day and they aren't going to dwell on that error in your slide. You shouldn't either. Learn from it, but get over it. The errors that are typically fatal are those that involve ethics, judgment or mistreating other people. You'll probably survive everything else.
- **Putting in *the hours* matters.** I know that's not always a popular sentiment nowadays. And I'm not suggesting that work-life balance isn't important. But I am saying that there's a direct correlation between effort and output. All else equal, the person who works the hardest gets ahead the fastest. If you asked most company executives, they'd tell you there were times in their career (especially early on) when they really had to grind. Life is complicated and you shouldn't optimize for one narrow aspect of it. But don't be naive about the fact that your effort level matters in your career trajectory.
- **Avoid the three kisses of death.** The biggest derailers I've seen befall promising colleagues over the course of my career are *entitlement, unreliability and deceit*. These factors can undo even the most talented people. Nobody

wants to work with a person who regularly demonstrates any of these traits. Be the opposite.

- **Be good at *meetings*.** Meetings are to business what games are to sports. So it's important to be prepared and sharp and have a clear game plan, especially for the Big Ones. Three tips: 1) Plan a few insightful points you want to work in at some point during the discussion. 2) Make sure you know why each attendee is there, and that you've thought through their individual objectives and motivations. 3) If your boss is in the meeting, make sure you come in aligned and well synched.
- **Invest in relationships, especially when you don't have to**. Never miss a chance to be helpful to someone in your network. For example, making a referral, writing a recommendation or giving some advice. It's typically a small investment of time and usually you usually won't benefit from it. But sometimes you will, often when you least expect it. One reason I got a cool job at Uber was that I'd helped a former colleague get a cool job at Uber the year before, and then she sent my resume to the right person when this job opened up. The world is smaller than you think. Create some goodwill for yourself.

Those are some of my favorite career hacks. Ask your friends and colleagues for more ideas, as most people develop lists of their own over time. And make sure you share some of your hidden gems and hacks in return, of course!

RECRUITING

Whether you're coaching a baseball squad or managing a team at work, recruiting is a key ingredient to success. Talent acquisition is the lifeblood of any organization. Making good hiring decisions enhances our performance and culture. It is the foundation of competitive advantage and differentiation. So let's explore it.

Over the course of my career, I've hired hundreds of leaders and interviewed thousands. Although it can sometimes be a grind, it can also be incredibly rewarding. One of the things I'm most proud of at Uber is the amazing talent we've recruited internally and externally.

But even after all those interviews, I still find the process of assessing talent to be nebulous and imperfect. In the NFL draft, a process in which huge amounts of stats and film are available, over 50% of first-round draft picks turn out to be busts. Business hiring is even tougher since there are fewer objective factors to consider. I don't have a magic formula, but I can share a few ideas. Hopefully some of these will be valuable whether you're doing the recruiting or you're interviewing for a new role.

Philosophy:

- When drafting for a little-league baseball team, an approach that often works well is to *pick the best available athlete*, regardless of which position that person plays. Factors like speed, coordination and hustle are innate and can't be coached. You can teach a talented young athlete how to pitch. Know what skills you need to hire for and what skills you can develop. Of course that changes as athletes get older, and experience starts to trump innate ability.
- Preparation matters a lot. It provides evidence of interest and aptitude. A candidate who hasn't used our products and spent time thinking about how they'd approach the role isn't going to get far with me. I don't want them to just tell me about a frustration from their last Uber trip. I want to hear about their experience becoming a driver and how they would improve it if they worked here.
- Nothing derails the success of a basketball team like having too many prima donnas or superstars. I look for team players who will fit into our collaborative culture. A good way to assess this is by probing for pragmatic examples of teamwork. Also, my mindset is that I'm hiring for Uber, not just Community Operations. That means prioritizing candidates who seem agile and adaptable so they'll grow with Uber over time and build a career here.
- I love referrals. Interviewing is an imperfect science. When someone I know and respect tells me they've personally worked with someone that they think would be great in a role, it carries a lot of weight.

- Diverse interview panels interviewing diverse candidate pools yields the best recruiting outcomes, and helps us build teams that have the most impact with our customers, culture and results. It is well worth the effort to ensure every search prioritizes diversity.
- Don't rush it. Hiring is high stakes. Mistakes are hard to unwind. Take the time to make good decisions, and trust your instincts when something doesn't feel right. But be careful not to set the bar at a level where nobody can clear it.
- Make sure candidates have a positive experience. A warm and smooth interview process makes it more likely your preferred candidate will accept the role if it's offered. But even for candidates we decline, a positive recruiting experience helps our brand and reputation. Most candidates are also Uber customers.

Tactics:

- Make sure interviewers know their role in terms of what to evaluate the candidate for. That way you'll cover more ground and get a holistic view of the candidate. For example, you might assign one interviewer to probe for analytic strength, another for customer focus and a third for leadership style.
- In my initial interview, I do a lot of resume checking. I want to truly understand what candidates have done, what they have achieved and what experiences they have collected. A lot of people inflate their resumes, so I kick

the tires pretty hard. I'm leery of answers that start with what "we" did. I keep asking "What did *you* do?"

- I want to see tangible examples of success and impact, broadly defined. Past results are a good indicator of future performance. I want specifics and details. Don't be afraid to probe until you truly understand precisely what the candidate accomplished and how. Keep digging.
- I prefer experiential questions (e.g., "Tell me about a time when you...") as they give me a better sense of the candidate's true capabilities and accomplishments. Once the candidate starts describing the experience, keep probing to get to the heart of the example and test for robustness. Avoid questions like "What are your greatest strengths and weaknesses?" Answers are easy to fudge and are almost always rehearsed.
    - Pro Tip: Ask for a second answer to the same question. Most candidates have a go-to answer for questions they can anticipate. Asking for a second answer will help you assess how well they think on their feet and the depth of their experience.
- I usually ask a mini-case question that is directly relevant to the job. The best questions are the ones with no empirically correct answer, such as "How would you prioritize cost reduction versus experience quality?"
- Evaluate candidates based on the questions *they ask you*. Do they ask insightful questions about the business or conversation fillers that just take up time? Have they

done enough homework to ask about company-specific topics?

A few more tips:

- Develop a sense for when you need to tone down *evaluating* and shift into *selling*. If you're confident you're talking to *the one*, evolve your dialogue to focus more on illustrating to the candidate why this role would be great for them. This situation occurs more often when previous interviewers have already provided positive feedback.
- Make sure to include business partners on the interview panel. Robust feedback and stakeholder buy-in help to set up new hires for success.
- Show your recruiters some love! These folks are working hard for you, and it can be a thankless job. Approximately 90% of the candidates with whom they develop relationships ultimately get turned down. They have to juggle complex internal and external schedules. "Thank you" goes a long way.

RETENTION

Let's talk about *attrition* or rather, as I like to think about it, *retention*.

When it comes to talent, Uber is a hot global brand, and we operate in several fast-growing and hyper-competitive industry segments. Our employees are often on recruiters' shopping lists because we have a reputation for developing strong operators with valuable expertise. The most important part of my job is to ensure that Uber is creating an environment that will attract and develop great people. "External pull" is *a feature, not a bug* of working here.

The tough thing about having options is that it means our employees have to make tough choices. Their decisions about the place they dedicate so much of their time, energy and passion to is a big one. So it's well worth some introspection and scrutiny.

I'll start by sharing some of the factors that have kept me at Uber, and that are also some of the things I talk to other people about when they ask me for career advice. The things I find most compelling about Uber as a place to work include:

- *Uber is cool:* Your friends and family are impressed that you are part of a company that has so much cachet and sizzle. We're part of the fabric of almost every city in the world. We're a dynamic marketplace that affects peoples' lives in a meaningful way. Even my kids think it's cool that I work at Uber, and they don't find much else about me cool.
- *You can make an impact:* We're a young company in a fast-evolving space. There aren't many $100 billion companies that are still at a stage where you can personally move the needle. Here you can. Whether it's enhancing a policy that affects thousands of earners every day, strengthening a safety process that will save lives or doing an analysis that alters our approach to a key topic, I've seen relatively junior folks at Uber have an enormous impact.
- *You have career options and flexibility:* Uber has multiple businesses, vast geographic coverage and a plethora of robust functions. That gives you a ton of opportunities to gain new experiences, evolve your career path and hop your way around and up the ladder. You're not going to find that in a startup. What's nice about internal mobility is that you can gain new experiences and take on new roles without having to start over in terms of learning about a new company, reestablishing your network or resetting your tenure. That increases your likelihood of success when you take on new responsibilities outside of your comfort zone.

- *It's Glocal:* One of the things I've found most exciting about Uber is that it's both *global* (i.e., our business spans a hugely diverse set of markets, cultures and countries, which I find super interesting and fun) and *local* (i.e., our services are interwoven into the life-experiences of local communities, which I find rewarding and relevant). Not many companies operate like this, and Uber thus provides a unique level of opportunities for personal growth and cross-cultural learning.
- *You are learning things and developing skills that will be valuable regardless of what you do next.* That's part of the value proposition of working at a young, fast-growing and innovative company. You are going to see a lot more things, experience a lot more things and learn a lot more things than you would at most other places. That's going to be stressful and hard sometimes, but it also creates a personal growth accelerator.
- *You get to work with some really amazing people, and Uber teams generally collaborate pretty well.* We don't have the luxury of not doing so. Sure, bureaucracy and friction exist at Uber, just like at all companies. But I can tell you as someone who has worked in the corporate world for a while, Uber's level of politics and drama is well below the norms. Don't assume the grass is greener on the other side; it might be astroturf.

- *There is (considerable) financial upside.* You're taking more risk by working in a fast-evolving industry in which the business models, competitors and playbooks are dynamic and nebulous. The vision we are building toward across our portfolio of mobility, delivery and "moonshot" businesses will not be easy to achieve, but will be game changing if we do. With risk often comes reward. No promises, but owning a piece of Uber is probably going to be quite lucrative for you in the long term.

Of course, you have to figure out what makes sense for you. Over the past few years, a lot of Uber employees have asked me for advice about whether they should stay in their current role, pursue a new path at Uber or accept an external offer. People assume I'll have the answers. But I usually don't. Rather, I mainly just ask questions. I've found that the best approach is to help people figure out what is truly best for them.

In my experience, you should consider some key factors when it comes to deciding if you should stick with your current job or move on:

- Do you have passion and excitement about the company's business model, products and mission? Are you generally optimistic about the company's future? You aren't going to do your best work if you can't find meaning in it.
- Do you enjoy working with your peers and team? Having strong work relationships makes your job more fun and substantially boosts your odds of success. And it can be hard to replicate.

- Do you have a manager who is committed to your success and has your back? If so, that's a lot of tailwind; don't take it for granted. If you don't have it, it might be time to change teams at least.
- Can you name three other positions at your company that you'd be excited about doing within the next few years? If so, figure out what it would take for you to become a viable candidate for them. If not, you probably need to look more broadly.
- Is there more you hope to accomplish in your current role, and do you feel that you're still learning and contributing? If so, that's an indication your work is not done yet.
- Do you have a development gap that is holding you back? If so, that's a terrible reason to leave as that same development area will be even harder to overcome in a less familiar environment. Fix it first.
- Stepping back, what does your resume look like? Are you building a coherent narrative or a Linked_In profile that makes you look like a mercenary? A resume with a lot of frequent job changes could signal that you have trouble getting traction, get bored easily or lack commitment.

Career decisions are high-stakes and complicated. What's best for a colleague might not be best for you, and what's best for you today might not be best for you in the future. So don't over-index on short-term considerations or anecdotes. Play the long-game, and figure out what you truly enjoy and what makes you happy. When you're not feeling challenged, talk to your manager about what more you can do. When you feel like you're stuck, talk to your peers and mentors about how to reset. Get the facts. Assess your options. Know yourself.

PREPARING FOR YOUR PERFORMANCE REVIEW

Being good at giving feedback is hard. Being good at *receiving* feedback is harder. So here's some advice for the next time you have to prepare to have *The Talk* with your manager.

Reality Check: Over the course of your career, you're going to get some great reviews and some not-so-good ones. Some, you'll think are searingly accurate and insightful. Others, you'll think are utter garbage. But in the bigger picture of your career, any written review you get in one year or another may matter very little, whereas the actions you take in response could matter a lot.

Suggestions: During Your Performance Discussion

- **Don't rush through the positive stuff.** It can be awkward to have someone tell you good things about yourself. Most of us have been taught that modesty is a virtue. But if you've worked hard, you deserve some praise. And it's important for you to understand your strengths.

- Remember, it can be emotionally hard for others to give you developmental feedback. So your manager may be inclined to shortchange the tough messages. That's a problem because you might miss out on critical learning opportunities. So **let your manager know that you sincerely want to hear developmental feedback.** Tell her she's doing you a favor by being forthright. Make it easy for him to share things that might be difficult to say for him to say and for you to hear.
- The biggest mistake you can make is debating or arguing about the review or performance outcomes. Pragmatically, there is no upside in doing so. It ain't changing and all you'll do is come across as defensive and non-self-aware. But the real damage is that you'll be straining the relationship with the person you most need to enlist as a partner in your career development. **Resist the temptation to "defend yourself"** because by doing so, you're actually doing the opposite.
- I'm not saying you shouldn't probe to ensure you truly understand the feedback. You should. But do so from a place of wanting to better understand how you can improve, rather than questioning the validity of the feedback because…
- ...when it comes to performance reviews, **perception is reality.** Your review is a reflection of what people think about you in terms of what you achieved and how you achieved it. If you accept my premise that reviews are primarily a synthesis of perceptions, the logical conclusion

is that reviews are inherently accurate. Whether the Strengths and Weaknesses are empirically correct or not is irrelevant. A mind-bender, I know, but one with profound implications.

- Say thank you. Giving constructive feedback is hard.

Suggestions: The Following Weeks

- Put your review aside for 24 hours. Performance reviews are high-intensity events. Give yourself time and distance to emotionally reset before you start introspection or planning. Then read the review again, along with all of the peer and upward feedback. Take note of the patterns.
- **Write a game plan** for how you're going to approach your professional development. Put the same rigor into your development plan as you'd put into the plan for a critical project. Because you are your most critical project!

Here's how I'd do it:

- Put 60% of your emphasis on figuring out how you can further leverage your strengths. Leveraging strengths is easier than fixing weaknesses and it's usually more impactful. Sometimes leveraging your strengths means finding the right job. Sometimes it means building a team with diverse skills so that you can focus on what you're best at and delegate everything else. Sometimes it means finding clever ways to let your strengths compensate for your weaknesses.
- Put 40% of your emphasis on addressing your weaknesses. But not all of them. You're unlikely to be successful trying

to tackle everything at once. Pick one or two things that you think are the most important. Write a tactical plan with action items and milestones. Hold yourself accountable for following through.

- **Close the loop** with people who provided you with 360-degree feedback. Let them know you appreciate it. Ask them to keep it coming, rather than waiting until next year's performance review to share it if they see things you could be doing to improve your effectiveness. Perhaps even share your plan with them.
- **Enlist your manager as a partner in your development plan.** Make him feel personally accountable. Make her care. The secret to achieving this support is to demonstrate self-awareness and an earnest desire to continuously improve yourself. Most people want to help those they believe most want to be helped. Why? Because it's flattering when someone tells you they think you're good enough at something to help them learn.

I've received a few very difficult performance reviews during my career. And I'm super lucky that I did, although it didn't feel "lucky" at the time. Without that feedback, I wouldn't have understood my blindspots or been compelled to pursue personal development. I wouldn't have attained a true sense of the types of roles I'm likely to be successful at or the type of people I need to surround myself with to form a balanced team. Ironically, my "bad" reviews were actually my best reviews! Note: If my boss is reading this book, please don't misinterpret this advice as me asking for a bad review next year!

YOU HAD 'THE TALK.' NOW WHAT?

In my previous Coach's Corner, I shared some advice about how to prepare to receive your performance review. I hope your discussion went well. I hope your manager recognized your many strengths and accomplishments, and articulated actionable development opportunities. I hope the peer feedback gave you a clearer sense of how you're perceived, the things people appreciate about you and what you could do to be even more awesome. I hope the feedback was informative, but not surprising. Candid but not jarring.

You might agree with the feedback or you might not. Either way, your feelings are irrelevant. When it comes to feedback, perceptions are reality. For example, the fact that **you** think that you accomplished a lot of great stuff isn't going to earn you a big bonus. What matters is what **your manager** thinks you accomplished. The fact that **you** think you are a delightful person to work with isn't going to get you promoted. What matters is what **your peers** think about you as a teammate. That's how companies work. It's not a baseball game with a scoreboard that tracks the runs you scored for everyone to see. Perceptions and style-points matter here, too. Think Olympic gymnastics perhaps.

So now what? Mid-year review season is only five months away, so you better start preparing!

First, the basics:

- Read your annual performance review again. These conversations are inherently stressful and awkward, so you weren't *really* listening. Read through it again when you're feeling more relaxed.
- Follow up with the people who provided feedback to you. Don't debate them. Thank them and tell them you'd really like them to continue providing feedback throughout the year. Ask for help. Play it right, and over time you'll turn your critics into supporters and your supporters into advocates.
- Summarize and synthesize what you think are the most salient and actionable elements of the feedback into a bullet-point list that you can refer back to frequently.
- Write out your personal development plan. An **actual plan**, not just vague ideas. Don't try to tackle everything, but do make it specific with tangible to-do's and milestones.

Next, set a goal. Your primary goal should be *to make it harder for your manager to write your next review.* What do I mean by that? As a manager, the easiest way for me to write someone's review is to cut and paste what I wrote the last time, and tweak a few words so the duplication isn't as obvious. Most of the time, it's still 90% accurate. That's because most people intend to act on feedback, but then put it on the back burner. Inertia is a powerful force.

Here's what you can do to make your manager work harder to write your next performance review:

- Share your development plan with your manager to ensure that it explicitly ties to the development opportunities she wrote about you. Make sure she understands how you are going to address each one.
- Set up regular check-ins with your manager so you can discuss actions you've taken relative to your key development goals and get her to acknowledge your progress.

Now that you've made it **harder** for your manager to write your next performance review, let's simultaneously also make it **easier** for him to write it.

How? Write it for her! This approach has the added advantage of ensuring your review includes all your impressive accomplishments and highlights all of the awesome stuff about you.

Maybe you can't *actually* write your own review on your manager's behalf, but you can write a self-assessment that is so robust, self-aware and complete that your manager is compelled to simply cut and paste it into your actual performance review, thereby making the process very easy for herself.

What if instead of waiting until January to write your self-assessment, you **write it today**? You can list all the things you're *going to accomplish* this year, and articulate the strengths you *are going to forge* and the development areas that you *will overcome.* And what if by writing your self-assessment in advance, you can use it as a roadmap to actually accomplish everything you've predicted that you will? You can bend the arc of *future-you* by defining what you want to be and then day-by-day making it so. That's some true Jedi stuff!

In most games, there is a winner and a loser. But in this game, everyone can win. *You* win by continuously developing your skills, being recognized as a star and feeling good about yourself. *Your manager* wins by having to do less work writing reviews, forging a stronger team and basking in the smug afterglow of feeling like an *enlightened and benevolent leader*. Your company wins by building an ever-improving roster of homegrown superstars. The only ones who lose will be your competitors.

PUBLIC SPEAKING

Studies have found that people rank public speaking as a more pervasive fear than death. I'm not kidding. Google it.

Your leadership journey will inevitably include some public speaking, be it to an intimate audience of five or a company-wide summit of thousands. So, like death, public speaking is probably not something you can avoid. But the good news is that it is something you can make less scary.

Some people are naturally gifted orators. This advice is not for them. Similarly, if you aspire to be a truly awesome presenter, you're going to have to put a lot of time into practice and study. This advice is not for you either. If you're interested in learning about some tricks that have helped me, a speaker of limited natural talents, survive in a job that requires a lot of stage time, this advice is for you.

My advice:

- **Step onto the stage with confidence, even if it's manufactured confidence:** There's a strong correlation between how self-confident I am when I walk to the podium and how well the presentation goes. Rather than spend the last five minutes before showtime mentally rehearsing and second-guessing my material, I need to induce a rush of positive thoughts about how awesome it's going to go. My goal is to trick myself into feeling confident, even when I'm not. An audience can sense confidence, or a lack thereof.

- **Nail the first 30 seconds:** Getting off to a strong start is the most important part of a presentation. Why? Because it creates a self-confidence flywheel. More importantly, in those first 30 seconds, audience members are deciding if they want to pay attention to you or check their smartphone. You're competing against Instagram! Here's how I approach it:
    - I rehearse the heck out of my first 30 seconds. I mentally go through it dozens of times. It is the only part of my presentation that I memorize verbatim. That's because I know the first several seconds are the most nerve-wracking and I want to start out on autopilot until I settle into a rhythm.
    - I have a hook. For me, it's typically humor. I'm going to lead with something to get the audience laughing and naively thinking they should pay attention to the rest of my talk because it might be entertaining. Find what works for you. Maybe it's an emotional story or a cool innovation rather than a joke. But whatever you do....

- **...don't be boring:** It's better to be bad than boring. At least people pay attention to a trainwreck, and you'll be able to get your point across. So make sure you're not just reading slides. Modulate your voice. Incorporate some humor, pizzazz or emotional appeal. Remember, you are competing for attention with Twitter and Tinder.
- **Set visual anchor points:** Identify some friendly faces (i.e., people who are smiling and attentive) in a few different spots in the audience. As you speak, rotate your gaze across those three or four people, and nobody else. Since they're in different places, the audience won't figure out your trick. It will help you maintain self-confidence and energy as you speak. Looking at tuned-out people does the opposite.
- **Know your audience or audiences:** Think about what messages you're trying to communicate to which people. And remember it's probably multi-faceted. When I do a Community Operations update at a staff meeting, I'm trying to reach three audiences with three different messages. I want my Community Operations team to know their work is appreciated by the company and well-represented by me. I want the rest of the company to know that Community Operations is doing cool stuff and making a difference in the lives of our customers everyday. I want the C-suite leaders to think I'm a reasonably competent executive and unlikely to embarrass the company (much).
- **Use a clip-on mic:** Handheld mics are just one more distraction. Never speak from a stationary mic at a podium. It eliminates your mobility.

- **Do a walk-through:** Make sure your speaker's notes are working and you understand how the stage is set up. It's one less thing to worry about at showtime.
- **Slow down!:** Talk at about 75% the pace you think is normal. Artificially slowing down will actually come across as a normal pace. Watch the tape.
- **Close strong and don't linger:** Make sure to close with a key point and something memorable. Then get off the stage quickly, leaving the audience hungry for more.

Happy presenting!

ANY QUESTIONS?

You've been working on your big presentation for weeks. The numbers are compelling, the fundamentals are sound and the logic is airtight. You've triple-checked every table, graph and slide. It's your moment to shine, and if this presentation goes well and you're able to convince the key decision makers that your recommendations are strong, it could be impactful for your company and transformational for your career. So no pressure!

You take a deep breath and start your presentation, and before you know it, you're halfway through it and things are going great. The key audience members are nodding along and your boss has a big smile on her face. You see the checkered flag in the distance and can taste the champagne. And that's when the senior-most person in the room asks *the question*. You thought you were prepared for anything, but apparently not this one. Now what?

Business meetings are typically discussions, not one-way presentations. Questions and debate are an important part of ensuring mutual understanding, optimized decision making and getting to the best possible outcomes. Tough questions are an important part of that process. But that doesn't make it any easier when they hit you by surprise. So let's think through some strategies.

To be candid, the single best strategy you can employ is to **Be Prepared**. Make sure you know your topic inside-out, and that you have a thorough understanding of the numbers. Have a colleague with a fresh set of eyes review your presentation and look for gaps. Think through potential questions that could arise from each slide, and pre-think about how you'd answer. The bar is high, and the expectation is that you know your stuff and are well prepared. It is a compelling part of top tier company culture that even the senior-most leaders are well versed in the details of our business and like to dig in. You gotta do the work.

But even the most well prepared presenters sometimes get stumped. Another aspect of a winning company culture is that we hire folks who are super smart, and that means they are going to ask good hard questions—and that's a good thing. Just not for you in this particular moment perhaps!

Here's some suggestions and tips when you're stumped:

- **Take a breath and pause for a second:** Nobody expects you to have every factoid on the tip of your tongue, and sometimes the right insight will come to you after a few seconds. Buy some time if you think it could help (e.g., "hmm, great question, let me think about it for a sec.")
- **Clarify and probe:** Make sure you truly understand the question before starting to answer it. It is perfectly

acceptable to ask a clarifying question and make sure you fully understand what is being asked. It's often a good idea to rephrase the question and play it back to the asker to ensure you are on the right track. This also subtly buys you some more time to think about how to answer.

- **Root cause it:** Try to figure out what is at the heart of what the questioner really cares about. Perhaps the wording of the question is about a piece of missing data (that you don't have handy), but the intent of the question is to better understand the rationale for a recommendation (which you are able to articulate). Sometimes you can assuage the concern by addressing the underlying issue which gave rise to the question in the first place, without even having to answer the actual question.
- **Ask a friend:** Perhaps there is someone else in the room who knows the answer. If so, it is absolutely fine to let that person chime in. Nobody expects you to be the expert on everything. But don't cold-call on someone else as a way to shift the pressure off of you—that's going to damage important relationships, plus it's just not nice.
- **Defer it:** It is perfectly acceptable, and actually quite common in ELT level meetings, to tell the questioner that you don't know the answer offhand, but will follow up offline after the meeting. That enables you to get your facts together, and provide a robust answer with full context. I think this is an underused tactic, likely because we feel so much pressure to always be ready for anything. Just make sure you follow through and close the loop on important questions.

Those are some do's. Here are some don'ts:

- **Don't guess:** It's generally better to defer the question rather than answer with incorrect information. Getting the answer wrong is just going to deepen the hole and make your follow up harder. Plus it risks undermining trust. It's fine to say "I think…" and take your best shot, but only if you're 80%ish sure that your answer is correct.
- **Don't over-answer:** I see people get into trouble by providing very long answers to fairly straightforward questions, and going off on too many tangents. That just creates more confusion and risks creating a negative spiral. Try to keep your answers concise and direct.
- **Don't get derailed:** Chances are that not knowing the answer to one tough question won't fundamentally change the validity of your overall presentation and recommendation. So find a way to move on and get your schtick back on track. Mentally move past the glitch, and focus on the key messages you want to convey. When the shortstop on a baseball team makes an error, the most important thing he can do is brush it off and get ready to make a better play on the next ball hit his way.

One lesson I've learned leading a large function and as someone who is on the receiving end of lots of presentations is that *questions can be expensive*. What I mean by that is that sometimes when I ask a question that the presenter doesn't immediately know the answer to, it ends up generating a flurry of activity after the meeting so that the team can follow up with a robust answer. That time comes at the expense of other things the team could have been working on, and thus it has an invisible cost to the organization. So I've been pondering this dynamic.

There are three reason why I might ask the presenter a question during a meeting: 1) Because I think it is important information that I need to understand to make a decision or provide guidance to the team; 2) Because I'm just intellectually curious about something that I think is cool; or 3) Because I'm just trying to be polite by demonstrating to the presenter that I'm interested and paying attention. For category #1 questions, the flurry that goes into the follow up response is hopefully worth it. But for the other two categories it is probably not a good use of team time to do a bunch of analysis or research in order to follow up with me. So my learning is that I need to be clear when I want a follow up to a question or when I don't. I think this same dynamic plays out at all levels or an organization. I've seen examples of teams spending hours and hours of work to follow up on questions from senior execs that were probably just asked out of curiosity or courtesy.

That wraps up this edition of Coach's Corner… but if you have any questions, please don't hesitate to ask!

LEADERSHIP IN TIMES OF CRISIS

Note: This is the message I sent to my global organization at the height of the COVID crisis. Although that's now largely in the rearview mirror, I think the lessons we learned remain relevant and paramount. I've kept this column in the present-tense to try to reflect the urgency and uncertainty we were all feeling at the time.

It has been an intense few weeks as we've mobilized teams across Uber to respond to the global coronavirus crisis. These challenging times have truly illustrated who we are, what we can achieve, and the strength of our culture. I'm inspired by what we've accomplished and the speed at which we've moved. At the core values and principles that are guiding our decisions. At the tremendous teamwork and cooperation. And in seeing the power unleashed by so many talented people working together to do what is best for our employees, customers and the cities we serve. It has made me (even) prouder to work here.

But it has also been unbelievably stressful! Every day brings big new decisions, often ones that could have profound impacts on the health of our communities, the reputation of our company and the future of our industry. Questions without clear answers, and that often need to be decided with an urgency that doesn't allow for collecting all the inputs we'd like, or fully vetting all the options. My phone could ring anytime day-or-night about an urgent question that needs an immediate decision, the outcome of which could have significant consequences. Yikes!

If it's stressful for me, I know it might be even more stressful for many of you. I've been around the block a few times. For many of you, this is probably unlike anything you've experienced before professionally. You might be getting hard and complex questions from your teams, business partners and customers—questions that don't have easy answers, but that could have profound implications. It's stressful when the intensity level is *dialed up to eleven* for days/weeks at a time. Especially when everyone around you seems equally stressed.

I was reflecting about two previous crises that I've lived through. The first was as a rookie people manager in the aftermath of 9/11 in the US. Our world shut down, and when it turned back on, everything had changed. Chaos. Profound sadness. Instant recession. But worse was the daily fear about what might come next. My second experience was as a newish executive at a financial services company at the dawn of the 2008 Great Recession. Blue chip companies vanished overnight, the stock market collapsed by more than half and mass layoffs abounded. People were questioning if our way of life would survive.

These weren't the first global crises, and I'd wager that they're unlikely to even be among the biggest. It is not my intention to trivialize these situations, but I do think we need to maintain some perspective and sense of history.

Here are some personal leadership lessons I learned from previous crises:

- **Ramp up the praise and recognition:** People are working hard and doing their best. They're being pushed out of their comfort zones. A kind word of encouragement or a sincere thank-you will go a long way. It eases nerves and provides critical reassurance.
- **Be more tolerant of mistakes:** This applies to mistakes you make and mistakes made by your employees. We're all operating with imperfect information, short timelines and a clouded worldview. Not every decision will be a good one, but we need people to keep executing. So let them know that it is okay to get it wrong sometimes, that you've *got their backs* when they do and that you're eager to help correct mistakes when they happen.
- **Anchor decisions in values in principles:** When a crisis is fluid and evolving, we can't predict and prepare for every possible scenario. So ground yourself and your team in core operating principles and make sure decision-makers understand them at a deep enough level to apply them in a wide range of potential real-world situations. Have a plan, but recognize that it won't cover everything that could happen.

- **Trust and delegate:** When so much is happening so fast, leaders have to empower their teams more than ever. It is the only way that rapid decision-making can scale. Focus on giving them the tools and principles they need to operate and don't try to make every decision yourself. Make sure you're clear with your teams about the types of big decisions you want to make personally.
- **Leverage your star performers:** In times of crisis, strong players usually step up and massively over-deliver. Also, be on the lookout for new stars to emerge. Some might surprise you. These folks are worth their weight in gold so make sure you are fully leveraging how much they can help.
- **Project calm and composure:** Even when you don't feel calm. Especially then. Your teams are looking to you for signals that *things are going to be okay*. You need to help them keep things in perspective, stay optimistic and remain focused.
- **Practice *self-care:*** You won't be operating at your best if you're neglecting sleep, nutrition, exercise or whatever else is core to your wellbeing. Go for a bike ride. Go to bed when you're tired. Call someone you love. If you're sick, stay home!

A crisis will always pass. And when it does, we'll have developed new capabilities and processes that ensure we are even better prepared for the next one. But candidly, I hope it is more than that. Imagine if we applied the same level of hustle, creativity, collaboration and urgency of a crisis to how we operate in normal times, although perhaps turning the intensity level down from eleven to more like nine. We'd be unstoppable.

BUILDING STRONG RELATIONSHIPS AT WORK

No single factor will have more impact on your career than building strong relationships at work. Forging strong work relationships is also a key enabler of actually enjoying your job. As important as this topic is, it's probably not one that you studied in school. You can't become a good relationship builder just by reading a book. Nor is there an app you can download to foster relationship building at work, although I'm sure it is only a matter of time before some enterprising entrepreneur builds the business relationship version of Tinder. Until then, it's a skill you'll need to practice and hone.

For some, relationship building comes naturally. But for most of us, particularly those who, like me, are a bit more on the introverted side of the spectrum, becoming good at relationship building takes focus and effort. The good news is that it is something at which anyone can become quite proficient.

Here are some humble suggestions:

- **Make the time:** It sounds basic, but time is often the most overlooked component of building and sustaining professional relationships. We all get busy and thus, it's easy to let connections atrophy. Set up recurring check-ins with key folks with whom you want to maintain relationships. Be respectful of each other's time, but don't feel you have to cancel whenever you don't have an urgent topic to discuss. Also, don't rely entirely on in-person conversations. Forwarding a link to a cool news item or relevant anecdote is a great way to let folks know you are thinking about them.

- **Be a good listener:** Take an active interest in the people you work with by making an effort to truly understand what's important to them, what they are excited about and what is keeping them up at night. Ask good questions. Be fully present. You know the old expression: *you have two ears, but just one mouth for a reason.*
- **Identify things you can partner on:** The best way to strengthen a professional relationship is by working together on topics of mutual benefit. There is something magical about brainstorming, collaborating and problem solving that creates strong bonds. Partnering in pursuit of a common objective is a great way to foster teamwork. And the feeling of achieving something meaningful with a colleague establishes camaraderie and goodwill. It also creates a good ongoing topic of conversation and engagement, perhaps one that will even yield some powerful war stories or folklore.
- **Show that you care:** Again, we are all busy. And we all have a tendency to rely heavily on email, Slack and Google comments to communicate. The problem is that those mediums can come across as transactional and cold. So

find opportunities to sometimes add a few extra *words*. Check in to find out how your teammates are doing. Let your *human side* show. Just stop by to say *hello* sometimes. Most people will appreciate it.

- **Make yourself easier to get to know:** Even in a fast-paced corporate culture, most interactions start with a bit of chit-chat. If that's not a natural skill for you, use some *cheats*. By that I mean, make it easier for people to start a friendly conversation with you. Put a picture of your family, pet or favorite team on your desk or in your Zoom background. Leave a book you're reading in clear sight. You get the idea: give folks some conversation starter clues. And, conversely, look for clues that others give you about potential interests you can ask them about.
- **Be valiant about *trust and integrity*:** Broken relationships are hard to repair. And nothing damages a relationship as much as when someone doubts your underlying intentions. When you're dealing with anything that could conceivably be misinterpreted as an integrity issue, think through your approach. Err on the side of transparency. Give relevant colleagues a 'pre-wire' before you present something that might prove controversial to a broader audience. When you incorporate someone else's work into your deck, make sure to clearly source it. Provide extra *context* when you make decisions about things that might be *delicate*. When relationships fray due to integrity issues, the damage is often driven by misinterpretation rather than malicious intent. Which brings me to...

- **Assume good intentions:** The vast majority of people you work with want to do the right thing and be good colleagues. But we all have bad days. Cut one another some slack, especially during stressful times. Assume the best about people until proven otherwise. And when a relationship does fray, don't hesitate to give people second chances.
- **Ask for help:** Most people think the key to building a strong relationship is to offer help. And you should. But it is equally powerful to ask for help. Doing so requires you to be vulnerable, which can actually be endearing. Asking for help is also an implicit indication that you respect the skills and knowledge of the person you ask and that's flattering.

Back in the day, a big part of professional relationship building happened on the golf course, over cocktails or at a swanky restaurant. That's not really the case any more in most industries and companies. And I think that's a good thing, as the old way wasn't inclusive for a lot of folks. Socialize with colleagues in ways that don't artificially narrow the universe of people you connect with.

You don't have to be the world's most charismatic, outgoing or charming person to build strong relationships at work. What you do need is to make a genuine effort and that is very much within your control, if you actively work at it. At least until there's an app for that.

ALL IN!

I love the "sport" of poker, and my favorite game is Texas Hold'em. I've found that poker can be a good metaphor for many things in life. Success at poker is based on a mix of math, logic, strategy, intuition, observation, and a variety of people-related skills. Plus, admittedly, some luck. As such, the skills I've developed playing poker have actually been relevant in other aspects of my professional and personal life.

Skeptical? Well, here are some things I've learned from a few decades of playing poker:

- **Choosing your Game:** There's a famous saying in poker, "If you can't spot the sucker at the table, then it's probably you." What that means is that you should be selective about the games you play in. Avoid tables in which you're going to be at a competitive disadvantage or in over your head. And if you aren't able to figure this out after observing the table for a while, it probably means that you're not going to do well if you sit down. It's better to find a different game in which you think you'll have an edge based on your skills and experience. Same goes in business when deciding what type of career to pursue, which markets to enter, etc.

- **Knowing The Odds and The Outs:** Because the cards are sorted in a random order for each hand, poker is a game of statistics and probabilities. There are *the knowns* (i.e. the cards that you have in your hand or you've seen on the board) and *the unknowns* (i.e., the next cards to be dealt from the deck and the cards your opponents are holding). Success at poker is largely about understanding the probability of how strong your hand is at any given time relative to the other players, and the likelihood that your hand will become relatively stronger/weaker as more cards are dealt. From that, you can estimate your chances of winning the hand, and how many chips you'd win if you do (ie your ROI). These skills are also essential in business, as we decide where to invest and how the probability of success changes over time as we learn new facts.
- **Assessing Decision Quality rather than Outcomes:** There is a lot of randomness in poker. Sometimes you read the situation perfectly, make a smart play and lose because a card gets dealt that helps your opponent. And sometimes you make a dumb play, but get lucky and win. Over time, your winning percentage is a good indicator of your skill, but if you judge every decision based on outcome, you'll often draw the wrong conclusion since outcomes are impacted by randomness and exogenous factors. So you should evaluate your decisions on the

basis of if they were logical given what was knowable at the time, and if you played the hand the smartest way possible. The same logic generally applies when assessing business decisions and team performance.

- **Know when to Hold'em and Know when to Fold'em:** This is a line from Kenny Rogers' most famous song - yes, I'm a country music fan also. It means that you have to know when to fold a strong hand, even after you've put lots of chips in the pot, when you sense that the situation has changed and you're likely going to lose and don't want to compound the loss. And also when you need to stand firm, even when you know there's risk. We've had to make some big decisions at Uber over time—exiting businesses and markets when we realized they weren't going to work out, and continuing to invest into some very attractive opportunities, even when it was challenging to do so. The key is to assess each situation, and make the highest ROI decision.
- **Looking for Patterns:** If you're paying attention, you'll start to find that your opponents often play in predictable ways, and a key to success is to figure out those patterns and capitalize on them. Some players play loose and bluff a lot, and you need to counter that with patience and opportunistic moves. Other opponents play timidly, and the key is to keep applying pressure to win pots. Just like in most competitive business markets, it's important to truly know your competition's strengths and weaknesses, and thus how to compete most effectively.

- **Going *All In*:** Sometimes you get dealt a hand that you know is likely to be the strongest at the table, even if there is still some uncertainty or risk. When that happens, you want to win as many chips as you can, and the smart play is often to push all your chips in. Poker players call it going-all-in. It's risky, but has a lot of upside when you're right, so it is a strategy to use sparingly. At Uber, there's been times when we've seen massive untapped opportunities, and made very big investments, even before all the variables were fully known, yielding some huge successes.
- **Dealing with Ambiguity:** In every hand of poker, there are unknowns, risks, red-herrings, bluffs and diversions. That's what keeps the came interesting, but also what can make it maddening. Good players seek to use math and pattern recognition to reduce the uncertainty, but also realize that a certain amount of ambiguity is part of the game and needs to be embraced. It can even be turned to your advantage. The same goes for most of the challenging and complex situations you'll encounter in your professional life.
- **Maintaining Poise Under Pressure:** Poker can be a nerve wracking game, with dramatic swings of fortune, unpredictable cards, eccentric opponents and brutal beats. The best players are those that can stay calm and focused on calculating the odds, analyzing opponents, and making good decisions under pressure. That's true of many things in life, including work, career and even family. There

will be times of anxiety and stress, and knowing how to manage this is important to both your success and your health. There's no secret formula to how best to do this, and different approaches work for different people.

- **Playing Ethically:** You've probably seen enough movies to know that cheating, hustling and other assorted transgressions are not uncommon in poker—at least back in the Wild West days. Cheaters can sometimes appear very outwardly successful. But over time, they usually get caught, barred from future games and go broke—or if they cheat the wrong people, suffer even worse consequences! Success in the long term is about building a reputation as a tough but honest player, with a reputation for integrity.

There's a famous saying about Texas Hold'em: *It takes five minutes to learn and a lifetime to master*. That's one of the things I like most about the game. I feel like I'm always learning something new and developing my skills. And I think that's true in most areas of professional development and career success. So shuffle-em-up!

THE WHAT, THE HOW AND THE WHY

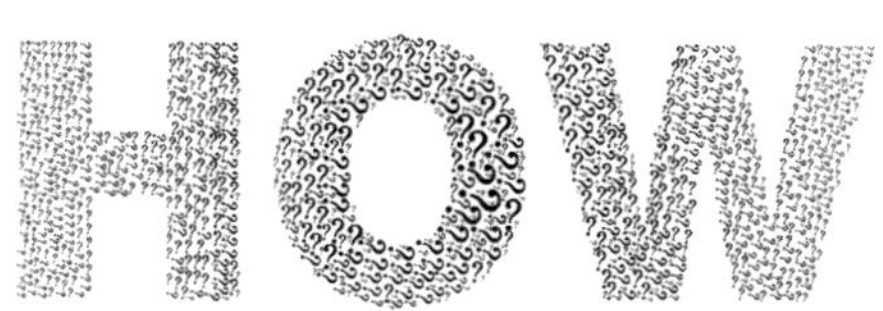

January is my favorite time of year. The holiday afterglow. The dawning of a promising new year. The Super Bowl is around the corner. (Go Niners!). And of course, it's the beginning of performance review season with all of its feedback forms, talent reviews and calibration sessions.

Perhaps it's because I'm still in too much of a holiday spirit (or had too much eggnog), but I'm going to spill a little secret about what goes on in executive-level talent review discussions. I've been in a bunch of them throughout my career at a variety of companies and levels. There is a consistent theme in these intense, high-stakes, back-room *people jams* that might surprise you.

You'd think that when we're discussing the performance, merits and potential of senior leaders that we'd focus mostly on *the what*. Did she beat her metrics? Did he surpass his goals? And we definitely do discuss those things. But that part of the discussion is usually pretty short. It's important, but not interesting. It's backward-looking, but not always predictive of the future. It's the ante.

The majority of the discussion—and ultimately what drives many of the decisions—is the assessment of "*the how.*" When we discuss team members or promotion candidates, we engage in much deeper debate about the intangibles of how each individual acted, led and impacted the broader organization. For example:

- Did she build a strong, high-functioning, high-engagement and diverse team?
- Did he collaborate effectively with his peers or did it feel more like he was competing with them?
- Did she inspire optimism and positivity, or cynicism and apathy?
- Is he someone people enjoy working with or someone who is tolerated because he gets the job done?
- Does she consistently optimize for what is in the best interest of the company, not just what is best for herself, her team or her function?
- Is he dependable? Does he maintain a high say-do ratio?
- Does she consistently demonstrate the values we aspire to as a company, especially in times of chaos, stress or pressure?
- Does he put in the extra effort when it's needed, work hard and follow through?

There's a reason why talent review and promotion assessment discussions focus more on *the how* than *the what.* And it is not that *the what* isn't important. It is actually super important because effective leaders need to deliver consistently good results if they want to keep sitting in the big chairs. Rather, it is that *the how* is by far the best predictor of the future of *the what*. You might be able to nail *the what* while failing *the how* in the short term. Or maybe just get lucky. But over time, leaders who inspire, collaborate, care, sweat and lift are also going to deliver better and more consistent results. *The how* drives *the what*. And that's *the why*!

You can be a terrible sports coach and still win a title. It happens quite a lot actually. Usually because you inherited a strong team. Sometimes because you got some lucky bounces. Or maybe because you cut some corners, broke some rules, burned out some star players and ended up on the podium. But you're not going to build a dynasty that way, unless you're Bill Belichick. To truly enshrine yourself and your team in the halls of greatness (see: Bill Walsh), a coach needs to relentlessly focus on *the hows*, the intangibles and the fundamentals. Do that, and the scores, banners and trophies will take care of themselves.

PRIORITIZATION

I love pecan pie. It's the best part of the Thanksgiving Feast. But last year, after a very long meal, I was too full to enjoy a slice. I'd made the rookie mistake of filling up on nondescript dinner rolls, stuffing and mashed potatoes. I forgot to prioritize my approach to the meal and thus, I failed to achieve a key objective of the holiday. But I learned a valuable lesson about the importance of **prioritization**, a lesson I think can be extrapolated to many other aspects of life.

Sometimes it feels like our to-do lists keep getting longer no matter how hard we work. And although it is awesome to see our efforts translate into big wins and positive momentum, we all still have a lot of important work to do. Fast-changing markets and leaner teams mean that a lot of folks are spread thin and struggling to keep up.

Prioritization has become increasingly important as a skill, strategy and tactic. When you feel like you have too much on your proverbial plate, the most important thing you can do is step back and prioritize before you (metaphorically) start eating. Otherwise, you'll fill up on the carbs and not save room for dessert.

Like most skills, the art and science of prioritization is something that needs to be learned and practiced. If you want to be good at prioritization, I'd suggest prioritizing these nine tactics:

1. *Make prioritization an ongoing discussion topic with your manager and team:* Don't assume everything your manager asks for is a high priority. Rather, ask questions and work with her to agree on the relative importance of each deliverable. Clarify deadlines and determine which might be flexible. Identify tasks that he considers "nice to haves" that could be a lower priority. Most managers welcome this dialogue, but team members are often hesitant to ask. So if you're a manager, remember to be proactive about clarifying prioritization (and reprioritization) frequently.
2. *Like Santa, make a list and check it twice:* Invest the time to get organized. You can't prioritize your to-do list until you actually create a to-do list. So before you start *doing* the work, make sure you've *planned* the work. Write out your key deliverables, timelines and steps you need to complete. Start each day by reviewing and modifying your list to ensure you are prioritizing the highest leverage activities.
3. *Identify what's urgent, what's important and what's neither:* A common pitfall is to over-prioritize what is urgent, even when some of the urgent things aren't actually that

important. If you fall into this trap, you'll fail to accomplish what's most important. If you prioritize everything, you've essentially prioritized nothing. If you're ever not sure of the relative urgency and importance of a task, ask your manager. Ensure that you're typically putting a disproportionate amount of time into what is most important.

4. *Learn the art of "good enough."* Some things need to be perfect, but most things don't. Look for opportunities to apply the Pareto Principle (or "80/20 Rule") which states that the vast majority of the value of a project is a function of a small proportion of the efforts that go into it, and a lot of effort gets wasted chasing the diminishing marginal returns of over-solving a problem. Sometimes *done* is better than *perfect*.
5. *Look for opportunities to stop doing things:* Sometimes we embark on a project with high hopes, but as we progress, it becomes clear that it just isn't going to work out. When you're feeling that way, step back and assess if it's time to move on to something else that could make a bigger impact. Talk to your manager and others who can be more objective. Recognize that there's an opportunity cost of continuing to invest time in something that's just not working, even if you initially thought it was a homerun. You can learn from losing.
6. *Prioritize within your priorities.* Just because something is a priority, doesn't mean that every aspect of it is. The same prioritization principles apply *within* major

priorities, and you want to make sure you (and your team) know what the critical elements of each major priority are. "The role of leadership is to transform the complex situation into small pieces and prioritize them," according to former Reault & Nissan CEO (and now international fugitive) Carlos Ghosn, a fascinating rabbit hole by the way!

7. *Obsess about your calendar:* Your time is your most valuable asset at work and at home, and it is a finite resource that needs to be optimized. In fact, if your time wasn't finite, prioritization wouldn't matter. Wrap your head around that metaphoric black hole! So manage your calendar wisely. That means being thoughtful about which meetings you schedule and agree to attend. Optimize your time by finding ways to go faster.

8. *Reprioritize as situations change:* If you'd asked me in January 2020 how I would prioritize developing a scalable mask compliance support policy or an operationally viable mass work-from-home ("WFH") capability, I'd have given you a blank stare. But these initiatives ended up being among Uber's top 2020 priorities. Prioritization is not a one-and-done activity, but rather something you need to periodically reassess as your life changes.

9. *Talk to your manager about prioritization rather than just making assumptions (redux).* Re-read rule #1.

Important, but often overlooked, is that you should take a holistic approach to prioritization. It's great to solve for prioritizing your work, but don't forget to also factor in your personal life. That can be especially hard when the lines between professional and personal get blurred. But it's critical that you're not ignoring your family, health, happiness and joy when you are prioritizing your hours, days and years.

USING YOUR SUPERPOWER
(A.K.A. MAKING SOMEONE'S DAY)

I have a small assignment that I'd like you each to do today. It is an easy one, and I think you'll find it will put a smile on your face when you're done.

I want you to make a mental list, right now, of three-to-five moments during your career when someone made you feel especially valued, appreciated or connected to your job or company. I'm not talking about promotions or bonuses, but rather small interactions that were meaningful enough that you still remember them in detail and reflect on them when you're in a rough patch or evaluating how satisfied you are with your job or how connected you feel to your company.

I'll start:

- Last year during a Business Review, I was sharing a challenge we were facing related to Greenlight Driver Hub staffing and earner onboarding. Dara sent me a Slack message along the lines of "Move fast and do whatever you think is right. I have confidence in your judgment."

- After a recent meeting, an executive that I don't work with frequently and didn't know well pulled me aside and told me how much he likes "Coach's Corner," and that he reads each one and forwards them to his team.
- A few months into my tenure at Uber, Travis had been pushing our team super hard to fundamentally overhaul a process related to a safety backlog. He had not been bashful about sharing his displeasure (to put it mildly). A few days after we cracked it, he came by my workstation and gave me a fist bump.
- In one of my previous jobs, a member of the executive staff had been quite negative and vocal about my organization. We had to help his team with something important, and it went well. Afterwards, he sent me an email, copying my boss and several other execs, thanking me for the work, acknowledging that he'd been a detractor in the past and saying we'd changed his perspective.

These were small moments, and I doubt anyone other than me even recalls them. But for me, they are vivid memories. What made these moments special was that they were personal and specific, felt genuine, came at an unexpected time, often when I was feeling stressed about something, were unprompted, and weren't from my direct manager.

The epiphany I had was that these people created these meaningful moments for me, and I have the same superpower to do that for others. And it was probably a superpower I was underutilizing. Like most superpowers, you have to deploy it judiciously so its impact isn't diminished but what a tragedy it would be to let it go unused.

Give some thought to how you can deploy this superpower in ways that are genuine, meaningful and specific. Don't force it, but don't be so casual about it that it doesn't happen. Put a reminder on your perpetual to-do list. Nothing will make you feel better than knowing you've created a forever memory for a colleague, peer or team member.

PLANNING

In October, two important things come to an end. The first is that the baseball season is winding down, and most MLB teams (including my beloved Giants) have been eliminated from contention and are telling themselves "maybe next year!" And here at Uber, as is the case in most companies, we're winding down this year and putting a lot of effort into planning for next year.

It seems like a good time to write about Planning, as many of us are very focused on that topic right now. I've found that some of the lessons I learned from coaching sports teams are more broadly relevant to planning, whether it is planning for next season or for next year. Here's my advice:

- **Reflect on the season that is ending:** It's tempting to forget about last year given all the energy around next year, but doing so will deprive your teams of important lessons that can help you win next year. Don't obsess about last season, but do make sure to learn from it.
    - Take a hard look at your stats and key performance indicators from last season. Don't focus on what the

numbers were; focus on why they were what they were. Think about what you might do differently with the benefit of hindsight.

  - Figure out which players on your team contributed the most, and make sure you have them signed up and excited to return next season. And also identify the positions in which you have key gaps that you need to fill.
  - Take a moment to take stock of your competition. Who bested you this year and why? Figure out your competitor's strengths that you want to try to replicate and their weaknesses that you want to try to exploit. See if you can predict what they are planning for next year and counter-plan around it.

- **Evolve the plan rather than starting from scratch:** You aren't going to change your team's fundamentals, capabilities or long-term plan overnight. It's generally best to course correct rather than start over since most strategies and tactics take time to play out. The arbitrary changing of a calendar page doesn't completely reset the status quo.
  - Identify the tactics that are going well, and figure out how you will invest more in them in the new year. In football, that might mean adding a few more running plays to fully leverage an athletic quarterback. In Community Operations, that might mean doubling-down on the proactive outreach efforts that are helping to bring more drivers onto the Uber platform.

    - Figure out which tactics aren't working and need to be jettisoned. In basketball, that might mean shooting fewer (or more) long-range shots. At Uber, that might mean pivoting resources away from products that aren't finding a market.
    - Find some exciting new ideas to pursue. In softball, that might mean adding some power hitters to the line-up. In Community Operations, that might mean developing a more robust approach to segmentation and differentiation.

- **Know your budget:** Whether you're building a soccer team or a business plan, you have to know how much money you have to spend and how many roster spots you have available to fill so you can make the right trade-offs and prioritize your investments. Start working on the numbers early in the planning process.
- **Talk to your manager:** Get input from your boss before you get too far down the planning-process road. That will help to ensure your plan aligns with the broader vision for your team and company and help drive alignment across the organization.
- **Start early:** If you wait until Game 1 of the next season to start organizing your team and developing your plan, you're going to lose a lot of games before you figure things out. So you need to start planning for next year as soon as the last game of this year ends. Use the off-season to get your team in shape. Likewise, if you don't start planning

for the new year early in the fourth quarter of the previous year, January will arrive and you won't have a plan. Now is the time to figure out next year.

Planning probably won't be the most exciting topic you'll work on this year. Yes, planning can be a bit less thrilling than playing the game. But going into a new season or year with a well-thought out and compelling plan and then ensuring your entire team is aligned and coordinated in terms of executing it can be the difference between playing for a championship and sitting at home watching other teams play for the trophy.

HOW TO SUCCEED AT UBER (AND MOST OTHER PLACES)

There are many core capabilities and skills that a soccer (a.k.a. football) player needs to succeed at an elite level. Speed, coordination, strength and work ethic are critical if you hope to make any national team. But beyond these foundations, each national team takes a slightly different approach to winning, and as a result, places greater relative emphasis on building a roster of players with the unique skills that best mesh with their game plans. For example, earning a spot for Brazil requires the ability to play with creativity and flair whereas playing for the U.S. Women's National Team is going to take a lot of grit, hustle and heart.

The same dynamic exists in business. Career success is largely a function of capabilities in things like problem-solving, collaboration, people management, plus, of course, hard work and accumulated relevant expertise. However, every company has unique elements in its culture, strategy and plans, which means the ingredients essential to career success will differ a bit based on the logo on your uniform or ID badge.

During my years at Uber, I've seen a lot of talented folks come and go. I've noticed some commonalities and patterns among people who thrive here. And the characteristics that correlate to career success and impact at Uber generally hold across most Uber organizations, job families, management levels and locations. Perhaps it's just stuff that has worked its way into our company's DNA.

You can probably see where this is heading. Without further ado, here is my completely unscientific list of attributes that I've seen virtually every truly successful Uber team member exhibit in one way or another.

- **Know the details:** We have a lot of presentations at Uber (Business Reviews, Operations Reviews, Tech Reviews). Most companies do. But Uber readouts feel different than other places I've worked in one key way: appetite for details. Uber leaders want to see the specifics and understand *the math*. This appetite doesn't diminish as you go up the management levels. Presenters who respond to hard questions with empirically based and detailed answers get noticed.
- **Be good at math:** We're an analytically obsessed company, usually for better, sometimes for worse. You have to be able to speak the language of numbers, even if it means dusting off your old statistics textbook once in a while.
- **Fungibility:** Because Uber is inventing a new market and industry as we go, versatility and adaptability tend to be valued more highly here than specific expertise. After all,

it's hard to be an expert on a product that didn't exist a minute ago. People who are plug-and-play tend to excel since they can quickly fill organizational needs.

- **Have a high Say:Do Ratio:** I've consistently seen a high correlation between people who are known for *getting stuff done* and people who are featured on our promotion announcements. And there's not much reprieve for people who routinely fail to make good on their commitments.
- **Be able to influence without authority:** Uber is very big, very global and very complex. That means our organizational structures are often matrices embedded within matrices. People who can work the matrix to successfully align diverse stakeholders and achieve results, even when they don't personally control all the levers, do well here.
- **Manage your own career:** We're not GE, in that there aren't secret committees constantly evaluating you and plotting out your career for you. Uber is still pretty early in its journey as a company. Those who succeed here tend to find their own ways and make their own opportunities rather than wait to be told what's next for them.
- **Love the product:** Employees who spend a lot of time using the product (i.e., driving, delivering and testing) tend to do well here. It's not about the optics. It's about a legitimate feeling that the stuff we build is super cool. To truly understand something, you have to immerse yourself in it.

- **Resiliency:** Our industry and competitors are tougher than most. We're going to take some hard losses. People who can't quickly get up and dust themselves off probably aren't going to find this environment amenable. Along similar lines, a key to succeeding at Uber is being comfortable with ambiguity.
- **Don't be a jerk:** I don't think it is necessary to be nice to succeed here, although it is nice if you are. But I do think there is still some aversion to the "brilliant jerk" archetype that (fairly or unfairly) got attributed to our culture during some of the darker days. As such, our tolerance for the "brilliant jerk" type of behavior is lower than at many other companies.

These attributes would probably be valued at any company or in any endeavor. My point is just that they seem to be especially important here at Uber. And because of that, they are things I look for when considering whom to add to the team or entrust with critical roles.

For most of us, it is probably too late in life to dream of scoring a goal for our national team in the next World Cup, although personally, I'm holding out hope that science will develop a solution so I can defy those odds and win one someday. But in case that doesn't work out for any of us, I'd encourage you to double down on the winning attributes that will drive your career success right here!

SEIZING THE MOMENT

This chapter isn't about budgets, expense management or tactics. It is about YOU, and some things you might want to be thinking about during turbulent and uncertain times. Don't let (hidden) opportunities go to waste!

Personally, my most meaningful learning and development opportunities came during some of the most choppy markets. And, perhaps counterintuitively, my career actually advanced much faster during bad economies. My hunch is that you'd hear similar stories from other senior leaders who have been through a few economic cycles.

As the proverb says, *rough seas make for better sailors*. Paradoxically, a company-wide emphasis on financial discipline and prioritization means that the growth opportunities for you —should you choose to seize them—have perhaps never been greater. Why?

- The company scaled back our hiring plans, but not aspirations. So do the math. Your company has a similar number of exciting opportunities to pursue, but is no longer able to just hire a lot more people to pursue them.

Ipso facto, there are more chances for you to take on stretch assignments to demonstrate to yourself and your manager what you're capable of.

- The initiatives companies prioritize and the problems they need to solve are going to be more profound in a period of market uncertainty and constrained capacity. So you're more likely to be working on truly move-the-needle-type stuff.
- Managerial spans are likely to increase and organizational layers are likely to decrease as companies optimize to new headcount budgets. So if you're a manager, that might mean taking on more scope at times. And it also might mean your manager is stretched, and thus looking for you to demonstrate more autonomy. In addition, Your work is likely to get more visibility in a constrained environment. The vertical and horizontal sight-lines are clearer.

Here are some thoughts on how you can accelerate your professional development, impact and career during challenging economic times.

- *Be Proactive:* Identify important things that aren't getting done and volunteer to do them. Talk with your manager about ways you could take on more or help out with things that are suffering from lack of capacity.
- *Find ways to be helpful:* Based on whatever your unique skills and strengths are, find ways to be a peer coach to teammates who might be stretched and would benefit

from your support. By doing so, you subtly demonstrate that you are a clubhouse leader.

- *Get with the plot:* Find out what your company's top priority is. Regardless of your specific function, program or initiative, make sure you can make a direct contribution to that top priority.
- *Put in some extra effort:* This advice probably isn't right for everyone since we all have different life priorities at any given time and putting in extra time at work might mean making some sacrifices and tradeoffs at home. That said, the return on investment for time invested is likely going to be pretty darn high when your company is facing difficult market or economic conditions. Drive in the passing lane for a while.
- *Be easy to manage:* What I mean by this is that your manager might be as stretched and stressed as you are. So anything you can do to take stuff off her plate and demonstrate that you're someone who can get stuff done without creating a lot of drama is probably going to earn you some goodwill.

It's hard to predict how long choppy markets and economic uncertainty will last. While you navigate the storms ahead, don't miss the chance to accelerate your career by seizing the opportunities that will abound to develop your skills and make an impact.

ESCALATIONS

"Cut it out or I'm going to tell Dad!" That was the war cry of feuding siblings in the Stevenson household. My usual retort was "The two of you need to work it out on your own." If I could have automated this response, it would have significantly reduced our family's defect rate KPI!

As kids, many of us were taught that running to Mom or Dad made you a tattletale or someone who couldn't handle things on their own. And sometimes that's probably true. But I also think we may have learned some of the wrong lessons about "escalations" as kids. In the business world, escalations are an important part of an effective operating and governance model, at least when they're done right.

Escalating stuff is a delicate topic. And it's tricky to manage because if you use escalations the wrong way, they can damage your relationships, tarnish your reputation or create an unhelpful swirl. When done right, however, escalations can be an effective way to resolve disagreements quickly and effectively, and even enhance relationships. It's complicated!

First, let's define "escalation." It usually starts with an *impasse*, which occurs when two or more people disagree and are unable to come to a resolution on their own. Impasses can range from minor disagreements about a small detail to complete misalignment about a major issue. An escalation arises when one or both parties elevates the impasse to someone else (typically more senior) to help resolve, block, mediate or decide.

At well-run companies with strong cultures, escalations help drive faster and better outcomes. At poorly run companies or those with toxic cultures, escalations are used as weapons. There are going to be times when you should escalate something and times when you shouldn't or at least not immediately. Similarly, when a colleague escalates something that involves you, you have to decide how to handle it. Remember, an escalation is not a sign of failure or disrespect, but rather a normal part of a healthy governance process. The magic is in how it's handled.

When to Escalate:

- First, it's generally best to try to work things out directly with your colleagues. A healthy and robust debate often leads to the best outcomes. So give each other the benefit of the doubt, and assume good intentions and competence until proven otherwise.
- It's okay to agree to disagree. If your disagreement is about something relatively small and/or subjective (e.g., Should this button be blue or green?), it might be better to just let it play out even if your opinion doesn't prevail. Save your escalations for things that matter.

- The types of issues that make the most sense to escalate are those in which a mix of things are in play: The issue could have a big impact on the business or team, you are confident your opinion is the better one, and you can make a persuasive case as to why and/or the impasse seems unlikely to resolve itself on its own.
- Don't wait too long to escalate. Once it becomes clear that you're stuck, delaying slows down the process, leads to rework and can actually make the escalation more fraught because most people become more emotionally locked in to their positions over time.
- Finally, make sure you have a crisp articulation of what you are escalating and what input or decision you need from the person to whom you're escalating. For example, is it about "the what" or "the how" of the issue? Do you need input, direction or a decision? Are you asking for mediation or marching orders? Being precise and specific will aid with efficiency and effectiveness of the resolution.

How to escalate:

- *It takes two to tango.* The best way to escalate an issue is to do so together with the person or people on the other side of the disagreement. That sets a constructive tone and avoids having people think you're going over their heads or playing politics. Think of an escalation as a way to get mutual clarification to help the team move forward, not as a forcing function to get exactly what you want.

- A mutual escalation may or may not be possible, depending on how the other person feels about the topic and the relative power dynamics of the relationship. Sometimes you may have to go it alone, but at least try the mutual approach first. And either way, avoid surprises. Always let the other side know you're going to escalate and invite them (or cc: them) whenever possible.
- It's generally better to escalate things one level at a time rather than firing off emails to senior management every time you disagree with a colleague. Start with the most relevant decision maker who is a level or two more senior than you. That is where most impasses get solved as the decision maker is still close enough to the details of the topic.
- Make it easy for the decision maker to decide. Be specific about the input or direction you're looking for. Use facts and logic, and don't try to influence the decision maker with prior grievances or emotions or by leveraging relationships. Present both sides, and especially the side you don't agree with, in a calm and compelling way. Otherwise, the decision is more likely to get reversed when the counter-argument gets presented later.
- Whatever, the outcome of the escalation, don't take it personally. Lots of factors go into decision making, and you might not always have the full context. Remember, escalations are not about winning or losing, they're about resolving impasses so that progress can continue.
- Finally, don't forget that most things in life (and at work) rely on long-term relationships, not one-off encounters.

You're probably going to need to continue working together after the escalation. So be gracious when your view prevails and diplomatic when it doesn't. Disagree and commit.

Escalations, when done appropriately, are a *feature, not a bug* of effective organizational decision-making and governance. Use them to solve problems, not settle scores.

Finally, for those of you with kids at home, enjoy being the Grand Mediator of escalations and squabbles while you can. It may annoy you today, but the time goes fast, and before you know it, you'll actually look back fondly to the times when your kids even cared about your opinions at all!

COACHING

Although in most sports, it's the athletes who get most of the glory (as they should), coaches play an essential behind-the-scenes role in molding great players and winning championships. As legendary UCLA basketball coach John Wooden said, "A good coach can change a game. A great coach can change a life."

Almost every athlete can benefit from having a coach in their corner. At their primes, Michael Jordan was the all-time best basketball player, Serena Williams redefined tennis greatness and Tiger Woods dominated golf like nobody else had before or since. You might think these sporting legends would have little need for coaching. What more could they possibly learn? But each of these athletes was passionate about being coached. It may sound counterintuitive, but the better you are at something, the more you can benefit from coaching. To quote John Wooden again, "It's what you learn after you know it all, that counts."

There are a lot of reasons great athletes benefit from coaching:

- Experienced coaches have worked with a lot of athletes. They've seen everything. They know what works, and what doesn't. They are experts at the-doing-of-the-doing. Coaching tennis is as much of a learned skill as playing tennis, although the latter pays quite a bit better!
- There's nothing more valuable than objective and candid feedback about how you can improve. A good coach can see what you cannot see about yourself and tell you what you cannot say to yourself. Good coaches can be dispassionate observers.
- A coach can give you a pat on the back when you need it or a kick in the butt when you deserve it. In the words of Ric Charlesworth, former Australian national women's field hockey coach, "The interesting thing about coaching is that you have to trouble the comfortable and comfort the troubled."
- Personal development is a continuous journey, not a destination. And like with all difficult journeys, it helps to have a guide to keep you on track and avoid pitfalls.

Michael Jordan said, "My best skill was that I was coachable. I was a sponge and aggressive to learn." This pearl of wisdom applies not only in the NBA, but also in Little League baseball. The players who benefit the most from coaching are those who are most *coachable*. Without a mindset of coachability, you're probably wasting your time, and even worse, your coach's time.

So how do you make yourself coachable?

- Be good at taking feedback. The more brutal and candid the better. Let your guard down. Seek the truth.
- Listen more, talk less.
- Suspend judgment and trust that your coach knows what she's doing.
- Practice hard between games and make progress between coaching sessions.
- Leave your ego at the door. Regardless of how good you are at something or how good you think you are at it, embrace the truth that you could be even better.

If you crossed out "athlete," and replaced it with "manager," "analyst" or "engineer," the advice would ring just as true. And that's why senior leaders are often the folks most obsessed with having a good personal coach. If the greatest athletes (and CEOs and CFOs) think having a coach is important, then perhaps so should you.

But that's where things get complicated. If you were on a sports team, a coach would be part of the *package*. In the realm of business, you'll probably need to find your own coaches. How?

- **Select:** Do some honest self-reflection and figure out what elements of your *game* you'd most like help with. Maybe it's public speaking, leadership, self confidence or problem solving. Then make a list of people you know who seem particularly strong in those areas. They may be leaders, peers, friends, family members or other people.

- **Ask:** It's only weird if you make it weird. Most people will be flattered that you think highly enough of them to want them to coach you on something that's important and difficult for you.
- **Act:** Work with your coach to set some specific goals. Identify situations in which you can take actions to make progress against those goals. Practice with your coach. Practice again on your own. And then again. After the big event, review the *game film* with your coach and find areas where you could have done better. In the words of Pat Summit, the greatest women's basketball coach of all time, "Most people get excited about games, but I've got to be excited about practice, because that's my classroom."
- **Commit:** If there's one thing I hate as a coach, it is apathy and entitlement, especially when it comes from the players with the most natural ability. I'd much rather invest my time in coaching less-gifted athletes who truly want to work hard, improve themselves and help the team win. This mantra is best expressed by legendary Notre Dame coach Ara Parseghian in the most inspirational and tear-jerker sports movie ever made, Rudy.

In sports, you're typically either the player *or* the coach. But sometimes you will be both, and your manager may expect you to be both. Surely you have some skills and abilities that others do not. We each have unique and diverse prior experiences. Find ways to be a coach for your colleagues who would most benefit from what you can offer. Give something back. Sometimes you'll find that the act of coaching is actually an even more powerful learning experience than the act of doing itself.

ACKNOWLEDGMENTS

As the saying goes, "He who steals from me steals twice." To the extent that you found some of the coaching advice or anecdotes in this book helpful, poignant or amusing, I'm flattered, but the reality is that my hard-learned wisdom is an accumulation of things that I've learned from the many mentors, leaders, colleagues and friends I've had the good fortune to work with, coach with or hang out with over the decades.

There are far too many folks to properly acknowledge, much less thank, but I want to give a call-out to some of my long-ago and/or longtime mentors, compatriots and coaches, including Bruce Schlesinger, Ian Frost, Katrina Helmkamp, Greg Zeeman, John Garabedian, Henry Vogel, John Budd, Neil Fiske, Carl Rutstein, Dean Nelson, Wayne Carpenter, Dan Leemon, Charles Goldman, Parke Boneysteele, Laurine Garrity, John Clendening, Wendy Larson, Andy Gill, Sherri Kroonenberg, Jonathan Craig, Rodney Prezeau, Naureen Hassan, Mark Jamison, Becky Saeger, Ben Stuart, Ann von Germeten, Rob Markey, Fred Reichheld, Aaron Cheris,

Stu Berman, Corrie Carrigan, Phil Davis, Brian Andews, Denise Leleux, Vicki Perryman, Scott Murray, Jean-Marc Codsi, John Courtney, Abbie Buck, Lynda Talgo, Joshua Rossman, Sherif Gayed, Zac Jacobson, Beth Axelrod, Carmen Orr, Wayne Bush, Prabir Adarkar, Manik Gupta, Liane Hornsey, Aisling Hassell, Todd Cook, Scott Scheinberg, Rick Lennox, and Cuinn Hamm. And to my editor, Marcie Geffner.

The source material for *Coach's Corner* has been a labor of love over the past seven years at Uber, and I'm thankful for the many Uber colleagues who helped me shape Coach's Corner content directly or indirectly. Special thanks to Deepak Surendran Pillai, Nanjappa Palekanda, Tamara Samoylova, Janelle Sallenave and Lisa Stoner, whom I've asked for feedback and input into many of these columns along the way. And to my succession of awesome Uber managers, Jeff Jones, Barney Harford, Rachel Holt, Andrew 'Mac' Macdonald and Gus Fuldner. And my amazing direct report team at Uber.

I also want to acknowledge the CEOs I've watched in action and learned so much from, including Chuck Schwab, Walt Bettinger, John Donahoe, Bob Swan, Carl Stern, Bryce Maddock, Daniel Julien, Amit Basak, and especially Dara Khosrowshahi (whom I've had the rare privilege of enjoying a courtside seat as he has evolved this amazing company into a world-class operation and iconic brand). And to Travis Kalanick, Ryan Graves, Pierre Dimitri Gore-Coty and Austin Geidt, who gave me the opportunity to join Uber almost seven years ago, to Frances Frei (the first person to tell me "you should turn these into a book") and to my too-many-to-name team members, peers and colleagues at Uber that I've learned so much from and continue to be inspired by.

I'd also like to recognize my former boss and still friend and mentor, Steve Boehm, who coined the term "Coaches' Corner" in his amazing leadership communications at eBay and graciously allowed me to put my own spin on the concept and take it forward.

To my family from whom I've learned a diverse array of life lessons, especially my wife (and editor) Barb, my dad Steve and my brother Brad who have provided some much valuable advice on leadership, personal growth and communications over the course of my life. Of course, many of these coaching lessons were thanks to my kids, Stephanie and Zach, who tolerated me on the sidelines for much of their athletic careers. And finally to those real-life players and coaches in the Big Leagues who have been so inspirational and entertaining to cheer for, boo at and learn from.

ABOUT THE AUTHOR

Troy Stevenson is the Global Head of Community Operations at Uber. He leads an organization of tens of thousands of employees and BPO agents across hundreds of locations in dozens of countries. His organization is responsible for Uber's customer service, driver support, onboarding, safety and risk operations, account management, and back-office processes. Prior to Uber, Stevenson was an executive at eBay and Charles Schwab. Previously, he worked for The Boston Consulting Group in Chicago and Auckland, New Zealand.

Stevenson holds a bachelor's degree in Economics from Northwestern University and an MBA from The Wharton School at the University of Pennsylvania. Originally from St. Louis, he is an avid cyclist, traveler, and San Francisco Bay Area sports fan. He lives in Los Gatos with his lovely and exceptionally tolerant wife of more than 25 years, Barb. Rambunctious puppy Mykonos is filling their recently emptied nest now that kids Stephanie and Zach are away at college. So far Myko has not expressed an interest in team sports.

Made in the USA
Columbia, SC
15 June 2025

0977811a-a15c-48af-9274-b7bd87b6dffeR01